JAPANESE
Etiquette & Ethics
in
Business

JAPANESE
Etiquette & Ethics
in
Business

FIFTH EDITION

Boye De Mente

NTC Business Books

a division of *NTC Publishing Group* • Lincolnwood, Illinois USA

1989 Printing

Published by NTC Business Books, a division of NTC Publishing Group,
4255 West Touhy Avenue, Lincolnwood (Chicago), Illinois 60646-1975 U.S.A.
© 1987 by Boye De Mente. All rights reserved. No part of this book may be reproduced,
stored in a retrieval system, or transmitted in any form, or by any means,
electronic, mechanical, photocopying or otherwise, without the
prior written permission of NTC Publishing Group.
Manufactured in the United States of America.
Library of Congress Catalog Card Number: 86-60830

9 0 ML 9 8 7 6 5

Contents

Preface

The reader is invited to imagine a group of some twenty men and five women sitting on floor cushions below low tables that have been arranged in the form of a hollow square in a huge Japanese-style tatami-mat room. The tables are covered with bowls, plates, and various other dishes containing the leftovers of a meal. In front of each man is an unfinished bottle of beer or flask of *sake*. The five women are geisha. While they keep up a steady patter of ribald banter with the men, they also see to it that nobody's beer glass or *sake* cup is empty.

Suddenly one of the girls shouts, "How about a dance? Come on! Somebody dance!" Others take up the cry, calling out various names of men who are in the party. Finally, the man toward whom most of the shouts are directed stands up, arranges his *yukata* (yuu-kah-tah) robe and steps out into the center of the room. He slowly composes his face into an expressionless mask, assumes a formalized stance with his legs apart, pulls a folded fan from his waistband, and snaps it open with a flourish.

His audience claps loudly and roars its approval. One of the geisha begins to pick out a slow, solemn tune on a *shamisen* (shah-me-sen). The man starts to dance. His audience quiets down and watches him in silence. He is grossly fat, with a stomach that bulges out in a ponderous blister. The flesh on his face has thickened and bloated his cheeks until his head is almost perfectly ball-shaped. His figure is grotesque in its misshapen stubbiness . . . but he dances beautifully; as graceful, if not as accomplished, as an eighteen-year-old geisha-trainee from Kyoto.

The dancer on our makeshift stage is the fifty-five-year-old president of a Japanese company that manufactures computer parts and an ordinary businessman by Japanese standards. But when considered from a Western viewpoint, he is a bundle of complex contradictions.

In one area after another, it would seem that our typical Japanese businessman has only one thing in common with his Western counterpart—the desire to make money and prosper. But even this basic assumption does not always hold entirely true, so it is little wonder that Western businessmen often find themselves completely unable to understand or explain the attitudes or conduct of their Japanese colleagues.

Their methods of operating their businesses are different. Their relationships with the people around them, employees and others, are different; and, at least to some outward appearances, so are their motivations. They live and work by a set of rules—compounded from a unique culture—that are not only unknown to most foreigners but also inherently alien to the average Westerner.

There have been tremendous changes in Japan since the country began intercourse with the West on a large scale. Some of the codes and manners of feudalistic Old Japan have withered away because they were completely incompatible with the new order. Others remain in only slightly weakened form to set the Japanese apart from all other people.

Not all of the characteristics the Japanese inherited from their unique past are bad or disadvantageous by any means. Quite the contrary. But a number of them, especially as they manifest themselves in everyday business practices, are particularly difficult for the Westerner to understand, accept, and appreciate.

American businessmen, especially, tend to become frustrated when dealing with their Japanese counterparts because our way of doing business happens to conflict more strongly and in more areas with many of the fundamental principles of the Japanese system.

Of course, the typical Japanese businessman is a product of the system he manifests, and to understand him one must know a great deal about the system. Furthermore, the foreign businessman resident in Japan as well as the executive who visits there must conform to some degree to the system. It is essential, therefore, that the foreign businessman know why the system exists and how it works.

In considering the Japanese from any viewpoint for any reason, it is vital to remember that they are the products of a unique civilization and that their standards and values are the results of thousands of years of powerful religious and metaphysical conditioning that were entirely different from those that molded the character, personality, and habits of Westerners.

The distinctive etiquette and ethics of the Japanese in business are natural outgrowths of these cultural influences and are bound up in a series of interrelated concepts discussed in this book.

Boye De Mente
Tokyo, Japan

1

The Cultural Collision

In 1958, after nearly ten years in Japan as a member of an American intelligence agency, student, and journalist, I became editor of the Tokyo-based *IMPORTER* magazine, the leading English-language journal covering Japan's consumer export industry. For the next several years most of my time was spent interviewing Japanese manufacturers and exporters, who were trying to sell their goods abroad, and foreign importers who were flocking to Japan to make manufacturing arrangements and place orders.

Being a third party who was accepted as a neutral go-between, I was made privy to the innermost misgivings and problems of both sides. While attempting to analyze the unique Japanese business system in the pages of the *IM-PORTER,* I was also regularly called upon to explain the attitudes and behavior of one side to the other during interviews.

I was thus caught up in an ongoing case of mass cultural shock in which the Japanese, recently defeated in a destructive war, were almost totally dependent upon developing and maintaining effective business relations with thousands of foreigners who knew little or nothing about them and, with rare exceptions, were not interested in learning.

Reacting in typical fashion at the end of World War II, the Japanese had redoubled their own efforts to learn everything possible about the rest of the world, assimilating anything that would contribute to their goal of rebuilding Japan. From 1945 to about 1960, most Japanese economic commentators

1

and many businessmen were convinced that their total national character would have to change if they were going to compete successfully with the outside world. Businessmen like Konosuke Matsushita, founder of the fabulously successful Matsushita Electric Company, and Idemitsu Oil company founder Sazo Idemitsu, who continued to preach and practice the concepts of Old Japan, were looked upon as anachronisms who would soon fade into history.

Dozens of companies attempted to introduce American-style management into their firms, generally with disastrous results. Two of the best-known examples of the failure of American management principles and techniques in early postwar Japan involved the giant prewar publishing companies, Kaizosha and Uchida Rokakuho. Shortly after the end of World War II, the new, young presidents of both of these companies went to the U.S. where they studied economics and management. Upon their return to Japan, they immediately set about implementing what they had learned in the United States.

Within a few years, Uchida Rokakuho was bankrupt and gone. At Kaizosha the senior director and other managers staged a coup d'état just before the company was declared bankrupt, ousted the president, made the outstanding creditors stockholders, and soon had the company back on its feet.

Explained the noted writer-publisher Shichihei Yamamoto: "The senior director [of Kaizosha] knew nothing of economics or management theories, but he had a firm grasp of the unseen, unwritten business principles that are an integral part of Japanese culture."

The conspicuous failure of American management principles in Kaizosha and Uchida Rokakuho, as well as in several other companies, had a profound effect on Japanese managers in general. Thereafter the majority of them concentrated on adapting their age-old patterns of thought and behavior to contemporary challenges—with astounding results.

The Way of *Wa*

It was not until well into the 1970s, however, that Japanese businessmen really accepted the idea that there was indeed something unique in their culture that gave them a significant economic advantage over Western nations, and it was not until the early 1980s that they began to feel at ease and confident in attributing their remarkable accomplishments to such traditional concepts as *wa*.

Then, suddenly, *wa* was on the lips of almost every executive who got up before any kind of audience, including his own employees, because here was a concept, sanctified by age, that he could really get his teeth into. It was endlessly pointed out that *wa*, the ancient word for the concept of peace and harmony, literally means "circle" and that the secret of Japan's economic success was based on employees and managers functioning in human-oriented "circles" (instead of the series of horizontal layers favored by Western management).

The principle of *wa* in all of its various nuances is now given credit for almost every aspect of Japanese management that has proven effective. As manager after manager explains, *wa* incorporates mutual trust between management and labor, unselfish cooperation between management and labor, harmonious relations among employees on all levels, unstinting loyalty to the company, mutual responsibility, job security, freedom from competitive pressure from other employees, and collective responsibility for both decisions *and* results.

Wa is also said to be responsible for such things as the almost total lack of joking, horseplaying, complaining, and drinking on duty and other nonproductive behavior in Japanese companies, and for the active participation of assembly-line workers in the management process through such techniques as *Jishu Kanri* (Jee-shuu Kahn-ree), or "Volunteer Management" groups. Each of these groups is made up of ten or so workers who meet regularly to discuss their work, as well as the jobs of those around them that impinge on their own output, and make suggestions to management for improvements.

The concept of *wa* provides the Japanese with an all-in-one philosophy/ethic for their business system that includes specific day-to-day guidelines. Furthermore, it is a system of thought and behavior that they do not have to go to business schools or seminars to learn because it is part of their culture. Major firms do, however, often require their new employees to take intense refresher courses in the principles and practices of *wa*.

There is nothing mysterious or esoteric about *wa*. It is no more than a deeply ingrained system of principles and rules designed to prevent conflict and to promote harmony, mutual trust, mutual help, mutual respect, cooperation, and so on—all traits with which Westerners have a nodding acquaintance. But there *are* profound differences in the way Japanese and Westerners do business. The most important of these differences is that the Japanese system, as inhuman as it can sometimes be, is based on human feelings and human needs and is intensely personal.

Konosuke Matsushita, founder of the world's largest manufacturer of consumer electronics, is widely regarded in Japan as the supreme master of the "Way of Wa." Before retiring from the chairmanship of his company in the 1970s, Matsushita codified his *wa* approach to management in seven objectives (which each Matsushita employee is expected to learn and follow). These objectives are as follows:

1. National Service through Industry
2. Harmony
3. Cooperation
4. Struggle for Betterment
5. Courtesy and Humility
6. Adjustment and Assimilation
7. Gratitude

One can begin to grasp how important these concepts are to Matsushita managers and workers—and in considerable degree to all Japanese businessmen and workers—by equating them with the role of the Ten Commandments in the Christian religion, keeping in mind that the Japanese tend to take Matsushita's guidelines seriously.

Businessmen as "Living Buddhas"

To understand Japanese management practices and deal effectively with Japanese businessmen requires more than a surface knowledge of the concept of *wa*. It requires an intimate familiarity with the Japanese character and work ethic as they have been fashioned by one of the world's most extraordinary cultures.

Japanese writer, publisher, and biblical scholar Shichihei Yamamoto credits a sixteenth-century Zen priest, Shosan Suzuki, with being responsible for the development of capitalism in Japan, and Baigan Ishida, a seventeenth-century store-clerk-turned-economic-philosopher, as the man who expanded on Suzuki's views to develop the economic philosophy and work ethic that still prevails in present-day Japan.

In his book *Nihon Shihon-shugi no Seishin (The Spirit of Japanese Capitalism)*, Yamamoto says that Suzuki* (1579–1655) taught a Zen-based social ethic in which people had to become "living Buddhas" in order to live the way he felt they should. He preached that work equaled asceticism and was in itself an expression of religious piety. He taught that an unbendable commitment to honesty was the first article of faith in the businessman's creed. He saw commerce, which was considered a necessary evil by the Shogunate government of feudal Japan, as a godly endeavor whose primary goal was to bring freedom to the nation. In his advice to merchants, Suzuki wrote:

> Throw yourself into worldly activity. For the sake of the nation and its citizens, send the goods of your province to other provinces, and bring the products of other provinces to your own. Travel around the country to distant parts to bring people what they desire. Your activity is an ascetic exercise that will cleanse you of all impurities. Challenge your mind and your body by crossing mountain ranges. Purify your heart by fording rivers. When your ship sets sail on the boundless sea, lose yourself in prayer to Buddha. If you understand that this life is but a trip through an evanescent world, and if you cast aside all attachments and desires and work hard, Heaven will pro-

---

*Shosan Suzuki was a contemporary of Musashi Miyamoto (1584–1645), a samurai warrior whose only claim to fame was that he became incredibly skilled with a sword and killed over sixty men in duels by the time he was thirty. In the later years of his life he wrote a small treatise called *A Book of Five Rings*, which gave his philosophy on how to defeat opponents in battle. The book was published in English in the 1970s for the martial arts trade. An offhand mention of the book by a New York newspaper columnist turned it into a bestseller among American businessmen, much to the amusement of the Japanese.

tect you, the gods will bestow their favor, and your profits will
be exceptional. You will become a person of wealth and virtue
and care nothing for riches. Finally you will develop an
unshakable faith; you will be engaged in meditation around
the clock.

In other words, adds Yamamoto, the businessman must
travel around the country distributing goods as if he were on
a pilgrimage. If one pursues work with single-minded devotion, he will become a Buddha. All work is therefore Buddhist
practice.

A former samurai and government official, Suzuki expressed the desire to conquer the world with Buddhist law,
with his social ethic becoming the basis for all societies and
serving as a national morality that would satisfy the spiritual,
religious, and economic needs of all people.

In Suzuki's philosophy any businessman who pursues his
trade to make a profit will fail. It is only by keeping the needs
of the consumers and the nation in the forefront of all thinking, planning, and working that one can succeed. Otherwise,
he adds, you will incur the wrath of Buddha.

Yamamoto says contemporary Japanese salesmen abroad
do indeed look and act like religious pilgrims as they trek the
world with their samples and sales pitches, and treat commerce like an ascetic exercise. In other words, the reason the
Japanese are such hard, dedicated workers is because *work* is
their religion, and in Yamamoto's view, it is this religious
attitude toward work that is behind Japan's economic success.
The Japanese are in fact filled with the fever of true religious
fanatics in their efforts to achieve greater and greater economic goals. Probably few, if any, Japanese would admit that
part of their motivation may indeed be a subconscious desire
to achieve Buddhahood, but they would certainly understand
and appreciate the concept.

Baigan Ishida (1685-1744) worked as a clerk in a retail store
until he was forty-two or forty-three. When he was forty-five,
he opened a school called *Sekimon Shingaku* (The Ishida
School of New Ethics) in his Kyoto home and began offering
free lectures every morning and every other evening. At first
only a few friends attended his lectures and he made no
attempt to publicize them, but word-of-mouth gradually in-

creased attendance. He began holding seminars three times a month.

Seven years after opening his school, Ishida gave a lecture at a large meeting hall to a standing-room-only crowd. A short while later he moved into larger quarters to accommodate the people who now flocked to hear him. He began to receive invitations to lecture in Kyoto and Osaka. His fame gradually spread throughout the country, attracting growing numbers of the samurai class as well as the nobility.

Ishida's basic philosophy was more practical and pragmatic than that of Shosan Suzuki. He taught that man was responsible for his own ethics and behavior and anything that contributed to the good of mankind was truth. He said that man need only follow his *honshin* (heart of hearts), or human nature, as a guideline. He held that social order and progress could be brought into conformity and harmony with the cosmos if people followed the precepts of honesty, self-restraint, and order. He taught that the inner order (the true heart of man) and the natural order (the cosmos) were one and the same and were linked together by form.

Ishida defended the role of the businessman, saying that the pursuit of profit was just and noble as long as merchants followed the way of sincerity toward their customers and frugality.

After Ishida's death in 1744, one of his disciples, Doni Nakazawa, set up a school in Edo (Tokyo) to teach Ishida's principles; then he traveled widely, lecturing to all classes and levels of people. Nakazawa's own disciples subsequently established twenty-one other schools to teach Ishida's new ethics.

In Ishida's system people were encouraged to find personal fulfillment in doing their routine tasks. A rational act done in the context of a functional group was regarded as a service to the entire community and, by extension, to the country. Work became a religious activity into which people could lavish all their enthusiasm and energy.

The Essence of Japanese Management

Yamamoto says the essence of Japanese-style management today is based on the seniority system, which has always existed in Japan but was perfected in the Tokugawa period (1603-1868) following precepts set down by the Ishida school of thought. During the Tokugawa era the employees of larger retail stores and wholesalers were divided into carefully prescribed ranks. These ranks were *detchi* (general employees), *tedai* (supervisors), *bantoh* (section chiefs), and *O-bantoh* (department managers)—all of whom lived on the premises. The next highest rank was the *yado-iri* (general manager), who did not live in, and the highest was *norenwake*, the head of a subsidiary shop or company.

There were three ranks in factories: *kozoh* (apprentice), *shoku-nin* (journeyman), and *shoku-cho* (foreman). After many years of service, foremen were allowed to establish subsidiaries, acting as subcontractors to their parent companies.

Both *norenwake* and *shoku-cho* could become independent by repaying the parent company for stock and any investment, as long as they didn't compete directly with the parent firm.

Apprentices received no salary but their needs were looked after, and eventually they would move up in the system and have the opportunity to go out on their own as independent journeymen or as bosses of subsidiaries. This provided them with the motivation to work hard, learn the trade, and be loyal to the company.

This system encouraged the proliferation of companies, all tied together in communal groups. The communal companies, as well as their employees, were bound by the principle of seniority.

Each shop or company was run as a communal unit in which the spirit of the community was the binding force. There was no need for company rules or regulations. Each unit functioned as a family, sharing responsibilities and rewards. Yamamoto notes that still today rules do not have a very important function in Japanese companies. They are designed and used to preserve the traditional consensus and seniority systems, somewhat like the Christian practice of invoking the name of God to guarantee the sincerity of parties to a contract.

Contracts serve only to support the system of consensus in Japan. If they go against the social norm, which is arrived at and protected by consensus, the contract is void. The Japanese *are* willing and do compromise where non-Japanese are concerned, knowing that foreigners are not bound by the system of consensus. But among themselves, detailed contracts are still uncommon. Their word is enough.

The typical Japanese company today remains a communal group first and a functioning group second. Newcomers are not accepted into the community-company until they have been carefully screened, tested, and trained in its ethics and morality. Once employed they are usually not dismissed for any function failure, but they may be dismissed if they break the communal standards and tarnish the image of the company. Employees are primarily controlled by group honor and the shame that befalls them for going against expected behavior.

Yamamoto says the company is the community, and home is just where they sleep.

Ishida's new ethics for seventeenth-century Japan did not relate work or commercial activity with politics. It was his belief that it was the responsibility of the samurai, the hereditary warrior class, to maintain peace and political stability, and that businessmen should not involve themselves in the political affairs of the nation.

Yamamoto says the reluctance of Japan's present-day business leaders to accept any responsibility for world order flows directly from the teachings of Ishida nearly 250 years ago. He concludes that the secret of Japan's success as an industrial nation is the communal nature of the functional groups within society and business and that the nature of this communal group is religious. When an individual performs a function, he serves the communal group and in the process is spiritually fulfilled.

"Thus," adds Yamamoto, "it is natural that an enduring organization will center upon an object of corporate worship, focus on a corporate objective, or be led by a charismatic personality that embodies certain objectives. And since this group is a communal one, employment is naturally for life and a system of seniority exists in one form or another."

As part of the religious orientation of Japanese management, many companies have their own Shinto shrines, and it is very common for leading executives to visit an Inari shrine (the patron god of businessmen) regularly. A top executive in the Japan National Broadcasting Corporation (NHK), which has branch offices and factories throughout the country, is a Shinto priest who travels around officiating at ceremonies held at the huge company's branch shrines.

Virtually all major Japanese corporations have slogans or mottos, many of which emphasize harmony, sincerity, and effort and have religious overtones. The motto of one Kyushu firm is especially interesting because it is very un-Japanese instead of traditional: "Use your head and show some sense. If you can't come up with good sense, make up for it with sweat. If you can't produce intelligence or sweat, go home quietly."

The Suzuki/Ishida concept of service is still of major importance in the psychology of Japanese businessmen, and in general they believe that any company whose primary motivation is to maintain its own existence will eventually destroy itself. The attitude of American executives that their primary role is to see that stockholders make a profit goes against the grain of the Japanese.

The concept of the role of the company president in Japan today also goes back to the days of the Shogun and provincial feudal lords, when the lords themselves did not stoop to engage in commercial activity but encouraged their capable retainers to do so. The lords lived frugally, encouraging the pursuit of martial arts and cultural activities, thereby serving as examples so the lower classes could achieve psychological satisfaction in their own efforts and life-styles. The lords left the administration of their fiefs to their subordinates, just as the ideal president today leaves the mundane affairs of running the company to trusted lieutenants.

Ken Takaoka, director of Japan's prestigious Modern Human Science Institute, describes the Japanese approach to business as a matrix of nature, culture, and modern technology. A systems and aeronautical engineer and the author of numerous books and papers on science, technology, and business, Takaoka says that a deeply spiritual orientation combined with a highly refined sense of form and sophistication has conditioned the Japanese to approach their work with care, precision, and excellence. They "strive for perfection" with religious fervor.

Kenji Ekuan, president of GK Industrial Design Research Institute, said in the *Journal of Japanese Trade and Industry* that centuries of practicing the arts of swordsmanship, calligraphy, judo, flower arranging, and the tea ceremony led the Japanese to develop a keen "sense of how things ought to be, of proper processes and conclusions . . . to judge proportion with a trained intuition, to reach beyond the arrangement of the particulars to a holistic order."

Vocabulary of the Japanese

There are other special words in the Japanese lexicon that are the building blocks of *wa,* words that define and explain Japanese beliefs and behavior. Without an understanding and appreciation of these terms, the portrait of Japan's dedicated, dynamic businessmen is little more than a shadow.

In fact, the bedrock principles of the Japanese system, in business as well as in private life, are bound up in a number of special words which refer to a series of interrelated values, motivations, attitudes, and practices forming the foundation of Japanese etiquette and ethics in business.

Amae
"The Oil of Life"

Which of these key words came first, or should come first, is somewhat arbitrary. I have chosen to begin with *amae* (ah-my) because it seems to me to be the pillar around which the traditional character, personality, and aspirations of the Japanese are built.

Amae refers to what, for lack of a better phrase in English, is translated as "indulgent love," the category or quality of love an infant feels for an absolutely kind and loving mother—*and must have from its mother to stay right with the world!*

The principle and practice of *amae* are certainly not unique to Japan, but the Japanese are apparently the only people (other than perhaps isolated tribes or islanders) who made it the primary essence of their distinctive social system.

In his authoritative book *Amae no Kozo*, meaning the structure of *amae*—published in English as *The Anatomy of Dependence* —Takeo Doi, one of Japan's leading psychiatrists, observes that while *amae* is the "oil of life" in Japan, the principle is generally unrecognized in the West, even though it is one of the fundamental building blocks of human (and animal!) personality.

In practical terms, the Japanese do not feel comfortable or "right" in any person-to-person relationship that does not include *amae*. By this, they mean a feeling of complete trust and confidence, not only that the other party will not take advantage of them, but also that they—businessmen or private individuals—*can presume upon the indulgence of the other.*

All people, says Doi, have a deep, innate desire to *amae*—to unload their troubles on someone they can trust, on someone from whom they can receive recognition and advice. In other words, we need someone who will relieve us of our excess psychic baggage.

In Doi's concept, it is the person who can "safely" encourage infantile dependence *(amae)* in its purest form who is most qualified to be elevated to a position of leadership in Japan. The leader, being utterly dependent on those beneath him, is least likely to mislead them because he would be hurting himself.

The *amae* factor in Japanese psychology, according to Doi's line of reasoning, is what accounts for the "childish" behavior often ascribed to Japanese adults.

Expressed in another way, to *amae (amaeru)* means "to mother" and "to be mothered"—referring specifically to the purest form of ego-less relationship between a loving mother and an absolutely trusting infant. Without *amae* in infancy and childhood, notes Doi, the child's psyche and personality are scarred for life.

In Western societies, growing up has traditionally been related to *repressing* the need for *amae* and eventually giving up its practice—a factor that is obviously the key to some of the profound differences between Western and Japanese attitudes and behavior, since they emphasize *amae* throughout life.

Doi proposes that the *amae* mentality of the Japanese goes back to their primal experience during the dawn of their history. Furthermore, he adds, it was "national policy" until the beginning of the modern era. He says that the traditional Japanese concept of peace and harmony *(wa)*, which many older Japanese still feel Japan is obligated to spread to the rest of the world, is nothing more than "idealized *amae*."

Shinyo
Trust in the Viscera

Westerners have often commented on how difficult it is to develop a close personal relationship with a Japanese businessman, especially in a short period of time. Besides the communication and other cultural barriers that usually separate the two sides, the Japanese are reluctant to extend their friendship to anyone with whom they do not have *shinyo* (sheen-yoe)—trust, confidence, faith. To the Japanese, a man in whom they can have *shinyo* is a man of honor who will do what is expected of him whatever the cost.

The development of *shinyo* comes about only as a result of a successful *amae* relationship with another person; and this takes time—not weeks or months, but years. The foreign businessman who jets to Tokyo on a two- or three-year assignment—much less a short-term trip—cannot expect to establish close, personal ties with his Japanese colleagues that transcend either his foreignness or his professional role.

The *amae* relationship, involving the child-parent-adult personalities in each individual, is a kind of "game" the Japanese play in all walks of life, between subordinates and superiors, and sometimes between equals as well. Each individual has to know which role is proper for what situation, who can legitimately play that role, and how it should be played.

The foreign businessman in Japan, not being used to playing the parent role with employees (or the child role if he is approaching a senior Japanese businessman!), is usually unable to establish the kind of rapport the Japanese expect and feel comfortable with. As a result, there is almost always an undercurrent of tension in employee-management relations in Japanese/foreign firms, and in meetings between Japanese and Westerners.

By the same token, Japanese managers stationed abroad often find that they can no longer play the parent role smoothly, even with Japanese subordinates working under them. The system simply doesn't work well outside the cultural context of Japan. Where foreign employees of overseas Japanese operations are concerned, the Japanese manager either keeps his distance or does his best to play the adult-to-adult role—an awkward situation at most because he usually has not had experience in adult-adult relationships with subordinates.

When pressed to go beyond *wa* to explain the high productivity rate of their factories, Japanese businessmen will often refer to the *shinyo,* or trust, that exists between Japanese workers and managers and between companies and unions.

Japanese-style trust is easy enough to define but difficult to copy. It is an integral and inseparable part of the whole Japanese system of virtually guaranteed lifetime employment (among major firms), long-term on-the-job training, promotions, and pay raises that are still primarily based on seniority, collective decision-making, mutual responsibility, a degree of company loyalty that transcends most personal considerations, giving young managers training in several departments instead of requiring them to specialize, etc., plus the vital point that managers are generally not isolated from workers and have traditionally been held as responsible for the emotional well-being of their employees as they are for their professional and technical competence.

While fundamental cultural differences make it impossible for Western businessmen to adopt the *shinyo* system wholesale in their management practices, some of the tenets are easily adaptable to any enterprise, such as training programs that would make it possible for managers to have faith in both the ability and integrity of employees.

Many American companies use some of their best people to review what other "untrustworthy" employees do, resulting in low morale among the workers, lower productivity, and higher overhead.

Uramu
That Hostile Feeling

When a Japanese subordinate's efforts to *amaeru* are ignored or rebuffed, he is deeply upset. In fact, Doi says that when a Japanese is unable to express his *amae,* the essential ingredient for the development of trust and faith in another person, a type of hostility called *uramu* (uu-rah-moo) emerges. This hostility, he explains, is manifested by a deep-seated feeling of resentment against the person or people (or whatever system) involved.

Enryo
Holding Back

When the Japanese do not feel comfortable with someone or something—that is, when they cannot practice *amae*—they practice *enryo* (in-ree-oh), literally, "considering (things) from a distance," a word you hear frequently in Japan, usually as *"Go-enryo-naku"* (go-in-ree-oh-nah-kuu), or "Please don't be shy." Doi adds that while individual Japanese themselves do not like to *enryo,* they expect others to do it. The Japanese *enryo* a great deal, however, because it is their customary way of opposing things or avoiding situations that might result in their incurring unwanted obligations, or in disrupting harmony.

In all relations with strangers, Japanese or foreign, business or private, the Japanese feel constrained to practice *enryo* excessively *because there are always barriers between people who do not have an* amae *relationship!*

Westerners generally do not—often cannot —verbalize the concept of *amae* the way the Japanese do because we do not have a specific, commonly known and used word for it. We are able to practice *amae* to a shallow but nevertheless important degree toward almost anyone, however, often immediately after meeting them. The Japanese, on the other hand, either ignore strangers and the outside world or maintain a hostile stance toward them because their ability to feel and practice *amae* with others is based on long-term face-to-face relationships.

Earle Okumura, a Los Angeles-based consultant on doing business in Japan, uses two variable concentrics (Figures 1 and 2) to illustrate the basic differences in the psychology and personality of Japanese and Westerners.

Westerners, as shown in Figure 1, have a large, thick inner "core" (psyche), with a thin, easily penetrable outer "shell." On the other hand, the Japanese (Figure 2) have a small, fragile inner core (psyche), with two other "barriers" designed to keep people at a distance. The first barrier is thick and strong; the second one is conspicuously thin and fragmentary.

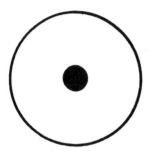   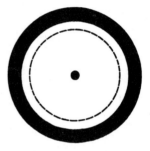

Figure 1. Westerner   Figure 2. Japanese

As the diagrams indicate, it is easy to approach a Westerner and get on relatively close terms in a short period of time—often within minutes. At the same time, however, the massive, solid "core" of the Westerner prevents the individual from really opening up, from dropping all barriers to the inner self. No matter how close Westerners may come, even husbands and wives, few of them can truthfully say they know the other person fully. There are invariably dark areas of doubt and wonder.

In contrast, the thick, outer barrier surrounding each Japanese makes it difficult and time-consuming to establish any kind of initial relationship. But once the heavy, protective guard is penetrated, the psyche of the Japanese is fully exposed—and extremely vulnerable to the unscrupulous person. The Japanese are therefore understandably wary of letting anyone inside their personal sphere.

Giseisha
The Victim Mentality

The Japanese, Doi continues, also suffer from an unusually strong, built-in susceptibility to injury as a result of their *amae* expectations—which give them an almost overwhelming tendency to become totally dependent on others. They experience this *giseisha* (ghee-say-e-sha) or "victim syndrome" whenever anybody or anything hinders or interferes with their aims or efforts. This feeling, he goes on, is most likely to be triggered when someone, some company, or some country on which they have been passively dependent, does something they feel is against their interests.

This "victim mentality," Doi adds, also carries with it an underlying need to get revenge to wipe out the "insult."

Chokkan To Ronri
Intuition vs. Logic

It is sometimes said that Japanese businessmen use *Jan-Ken-Pon* (Jahn-Ken-Pone) logic. *Jan-Ken-Pon* refers to the popular paper-scissors-stone game played with the hands and fingers by both young and old in Japan to settle questions or points of order. In this context it refers to logic that is cyclic or elastic, not absolute.

In general terms, Japanese thinking tends to be intuitive instead of logical. Doi also explains this in terms of *amae*. He says the Japanese cultural characteristic of attempting to deny the fact of separation of mother and child, and to emotionally generate a sense of identity with nature, is fundamentally illogical.

Of course, intuitive thinking is not necessarily or always undesirable. The management philosophy followed by Konosuke Matsushita, founder of the huge Matsushita Electric

Corporation (National and Panasonic are two of its well-known brand names), and many of Japan's other most successful businessmen, includes the use of intuitive intelligence.

Part of the intuitive process of this unique management philosophy is expressed in the term *kongen* (cone-gain), which means, more or less, "the root of the universe." It refers to the energy that fuels the universe—energy-wisdom that can be tapped by meditating, by emptying one's conscious mind of all thoughts and thereby opening it to communication with cosmic consciousness. Matsushita, regarded by some as the greatest Japanese businessman of modern times, credited *kongen* as the source of his management philosophy. Following his example, top Matsushita executives meditate regularly.

There are also many positive aspects of the practice of *amae*. It emphasizes tolerance, nondiscrimination, and equality. It also allows the Japanese to accept, absorb, and assimilate nonthreatening new ideas—technical, social, or philosophical—without internal conflicts.

The deep, compelling urge the Japanese have to *amae* may also be responsible for the powerful lust they have for knowledge. Anything that is unfamiliar or unknown to them—therefore making an *amae* relationship impossible—represents an unacceptable threat. It is characteristic of the Japanese, when faced with something new, to say, "We must learn everything there is to know about it in order to protect ourselves—and if there is anything worthwhile in the new thing, we will adapt it to our own uses."

Koto To Shidai Ni Wa
Circumstantial Truth

One of the first things that foreign commentators observed about the Japanese, beginning with Townsend Harris (America's first diplomatic representative in Japan), was their apparent disregard for the truth in the "Western" sense. Harris reported that they did not know the value of a straightforward and truthful policy and that they never hesitated to utter a falsehood when the truth would have served the same purpose.

Harris was regarded by the Japanese as a dangerous enemy agent, so it should not be surprising that an attempt was made to keep him in the dark. But many others who came after Harris reported the same thing, so it is important to look closely at the Japanese view and use of truth.

The "truth" in Japan has never been based solely on absolute principle but has been expressed more in *amae* (read "human") terms as something that is relative and depends upon circumstances and obligations. Just as obligation and circumstance change, so does truth. A primary rule in traditional Japanese society was that nothing should be allowed to disrupt the surface serenity of existence. When a Japanese was asked a question, his natural impulse was to give an answer that would please the inquirer, even when it was not true. If he did not have a proper or plausible answer, he would answer in vague terms, or give no answer at all to avoid telling a lie.

Another aspect of truth in present-day Japan has to do with personal responsibility, decision-making, and group orientation. The individual is often strictly limited in what he can say because he cannot act or pass judgments independently. This often puts a Japanese in a position of not being able to say anything about a certain matter.

Tatemae/Honne
The Two-Faced Syndrome

The concepts of *tatemae* (tah-tay-my) and *honne* (hone-nay), also manifestations of *amae*, might be called the yin and yang of Japan. They are invariably used in tandem and play a significant role in all areas of Japanese life. *Tatemae*, which figuratively means a "face" or "facade" of something, is primarily used by the Japanese in reference to masking one's real thoughts or intentions. *Honne*, on the other hand, literally means "honest voice," and refers to one's real intentions.

In virtually all contexts—social, business, or political—these contrasting principles are used to cloak the truth or reality of situations that might be inconvenient or embarrassing to acknowledge publicly. These situations can range from the innocuous, such as protecting one's personal dignity by pretending to prefer an old beat-up car to a new one when you actually can't afford to change, to pretending that progress is being made in an important business venture when there is none.

This kind of behavior is, of course, common in most societies, but in Japan it has been raised to a fine art and is an institutionalized aspect of typical Japanese behavior that one must recognize and take into account in all relationships. Foreign businessmen, politicians, and diplomats alike frequently run afoul of this Japanese characteristic and never know what hit them.

In business the *tatemae/honne* factor is perhaps used most often to conceal some kind of failure and secondarily to camouflage intentions that might prove disadvantageous if done openly. One example of a *tatemae/honne* action is when the president or chairman of the board sends a director of the company to take over a subsidiary, telling him, and announcing publicly, that he is the only person capable of handling the job, while the real intention is to get rid of a potential rival.

To contend with the tendency of the Japanese to resort to the *tatemae/honne* tactic requires personal antennae that are sharply attuned to the nuances of Japanese behavior and considerable skill in maneuvering around the ploy if one wants to maintain a working relationship with the individual, group, or company concerned.

Ignoring the rule of *wa* that says one will maintain harmony even in the face of such deception invariably results in embarrassment (on the Japanese side), then anger (often on both sides), and finally retaliation. A Japanese who fails to abide by the rules of *tatemae/honne* behavior is likely to be ostracized.

For foreigners not attuned to "The Japanese Way," it is doubly difficult to discern between a *tatemae* and the even more popular Japanese penchant for leaving things ambiguous (to dilute possible adverse repercussions from any source for any reason, to avoid giving the impression of taking an inflexible stand, etc.). In this case, the only practical recourse for the inexperienced foreigner is to call in a third party who knows how to penetrate the *tatemae* facade or ambiguity screen without ruffling *wa*.

The foregoing are not all of the ramifications of the *amae* principle in Japanese attitudes and behavior. The principle, one way or another, seems to touch on every aspect of Japanese life. Indeed, the structure of traditional Japanese society is believed by Doi and other social scientists to be an outgrowth of the dictates of *amae*. This social structure, to use the currently popular Japanese term, is a *Tate Shakai* (Tah-tay Shah-kie) or "Vertical Society."

2

Tate Shakai
Living and Working
In a Vertical Society

With limited exceptions, human relations in Japan, particularly the formal and professional, are based on "vertical" or superior-subordinate relationships between the people involved. There is, of course, nothing unusual about a society based on a hierarchical arrangement of inferiors and superiors. Most if not all societies are founded more or less on this structure. What makes Japan's "Vertical Society" different is that there is always one single, distinctive relationship between individuals and between groups—or no relationship at all. It is the character of this relationship, or lack of relationship, that underlies not only the etiquette and ethics of Japanese businessmen but also most of "Japanese" behavior.

The phrase "vertical society" was first used by Chie Nakane, professor of social anthropology at Tokyo University's Institute of Oriental Culture, in her fascinating book, *Tate Shakai no Ningen Kankei* (Tah-tay Shah-kie no Neen-gain Khan-kay-ee)—*Human Relations in a Vertical Society*.

Professor Nakane sees the superior-subordinate structure of Japanese society, based on an "ego-centered" ranking, as the primary basis for social order in the country—not only shaping attitudes and behavior but also overshadowing everything else: character, personality, profession, ability, and accomplishment.

22

If ranking in a superior-inferior structure is one side of the social coin in Japan, the other side is an equally deep and pervasive impulse among the Japanese to form themselves into and identify with groups on the basis of proximity and activity. Both ranking and grouping, as social and economic mechanisms, have their roots deep in Japan's culture. From ancient times, Japanese society was divided into distinct classes, clans, and occupational groups. Each of these categories and all the members therein were ranked on a vertical scale beginning with the lowest laborer or retainer and going upward to the immediate master or boss, the village or town head, the clan lord, and ultimately the Emperor himself.

During Japan's Feudal Age (which did not end until 1868), these group affiliations were mostly hereditary and rigidly exclusive, which meant that for the most part an individual could better himself only within his own immediate group.

With the fall of the feudal government in 1868 and the subsequent beginnings of industrialization, both the clan and hereditary class systems were abolished. In the next few decades Japanese society underwent profound changes, with commercial enterprises and vast government bureaucracies replacing the economic as well as political functions of the traditional clans. In this new, open-ended situation, the basis for grouping and ranking individuals changed from status by birthright to educational background and economic success in the marketplace. Neither the concept nor the mechanics of the vertical inferior-superior relationship between people was changed, however. It was simply transferred to the new bureaucratic and industrial order.

During Japan's long Feudal Age (1192-1868), this subordinate-superior principle was most often expressed in business contexts by the terms *oyabun* (oh-yah-boon), meaning "boss," "employer," or "master"; and *kobun* (koe-boon), which means "follower," "retainer," or "employee." Shop, factory, and restaurant owners; the heads of construction gangs; political organizations; and even criminal bosses were the *oyabun*. Their employees or followers were the *kobun*. *Oya* means "parent," while *ko* means "child," and is indicative of the connotation of these words.

From earliest times, the relationship between the *oyabun* and *kobun* was generally a long-term arrangement, often for life, and was intensely personal, incorporating elements of father-child, master-retainer, lord-slave in the relationship. Whatever the exact nature of the tie, each *oyabun-kobun* group functioned as a single unit, with the lives of the members and their families intimately linked together. The system thus had a stabilizing effect on society, politically as well as economically, and also acted as a very effective means of passing handicraft and business technology from one generation to the next.

In the *oyabun-kobun* system, advancement and authority were usually based on seniority first, and talent and accomplishment second. In a family-owned enterprise, succession was normally from father to first son or son-in-law. But if the family heir was incompetent, the ranking employee ran the business.

While the system thus supported and protected the less able members of society, it tended to stifle the potential of those who had talent and ambition but were not in line to succeed the master. Their only recourse was to break away from the group and start their own group—not the easiest thing to do in feudal Japan, when such behavior was either prohibited or strictly limited.

The *oyabun-kobun* system is alive and well in Japan today, although it is not always officially described as such. In many shops and work groups—and hoodlum gangs—the boss is still deferentially referred to as *oyabun,* and the employees and group members behave in the best *kobun* manner. Period films in which the *oyabun-kobun* system is a prime feature are perennially popular fare among Japan's movie-going and TV-watching millions.

Sempai-Kohai
Seniors and Juniors

In present-day Japan, the superior-subordinate relationship between individuals may be very conspicuous, or it may be so subtle it is difficult for an outsider to discern, much less appreciate. But it is there and is very powerful.

Today, the vertical, superior-subordinate concept is most often expressed in both business and educational situations by the terms *kohai* (koe-hie) or "junior," and *sempai* (simm-pie) or "senior." There is a word for "equal" in the Japanese vocabulary, *doryo* (doe-ree-oh), but it is seldom used because there is practically always something that makes one person inferior or superior to another. Equal business partnerships in Japan are, in fact, unusual because individuals who can function well together as equals are rare.

The basis for the *sempai-kohai* relationship is educational and economic, plus a time factor. It is specifically related to schools attended, year of graduation, educational level achieved, where this experience took place in relation to any other specific individual, the organization one works for, longevity with the company, the size and importance of the company or organization, and the individual's title or grade.

While the superior-inferior relationship pertains specifically to individuals in the same school or same organization (and those who *went* to the same school and work for the same organization), the status one gains from having attended a prestigious university and being employed by a leading company or government ministry carries general social status as well, not to mention the higher income it guarantees.

Although the individual who was graduated from X school, works for Y company, and has achieved a rank of Z in the managerial hierarchy is not obligated to behave as a subordinate in any chance contact with another individual whose school or firm outranks his own, he will most likely do so if the other person's superior "pedigree" becomes known.

The education/work-based, superior-inferior system in Japan thus touches every individual in the country one way or the other. Even the individual from a wealthy "name" family is nominally inferior to his senior classmates in school and later to his senior colleagues at work. Even if the company is family owned, he must behave in the manner prescribed for subordinates.

Kata-gaki
Rank Means Everything

The key to Japan's superior-subordinate structured system is *kata-gaki* (kah-tah-gah-kee), or "ranking." Everything and everybody is ranked, within whatever school they attend or organization they work for, first on the basis of their educational background, then on their seniority, and finally on their ability to get along with others, their personality, and their talent.

In the business world, as well as in a number of the professions, the specific rank of individuals (who have rank) is expressed in titles that usually end in the suffix *cho* (choe), which means "chief" or "leader." Over and above these obvious symbols of rank is the status of the company or organization in which the individual has rank. The higher ranking the employer is, the higher the status will be of any individual in the organization. This status is visually exhibited by the company or organization lapel button worn by employees of most major corporations and government bureaus.

Meishi
Who Bows First?

Relative rank between individuals in particular enterprises and organizations, and to a lesser extent between them and outsiders, determines not only the behavior but also the rights, privileges, responsibilities, and obligations of the individual Japanese. It is therefore very important to every Japanese businessman that he know the rank of everyone with whom he comes into contact. He must know not only the personal rank of any individual concerned but also the rating of his employing organization. One consideration here is that a section chief in a large, powerful company "outranks" a department head from a smaller, less important company.

This vital need to know the other's rank is the reason for the universal use and importance of the *meishi* (may-e-she) or "name-card" in business in Japan. The card tells the receiver the rank of the individual and something about the stature of the company he represents.

After receiving an individual's card (with both hands, while bowing slightly), each recipient takes several seconds to look closely at the name of the other person's company, its address, and his title, before beginning any conversation. Besides revealing which of the two persons is subordinate to the other, thereby establishing the level of language each will use, name-cards often reveal common areas that can be quickly utilized to strengthen the new relationship—office addresses in the same area, a relative who works for the other company or a subsidiary, and other such personal links.

Foreign businessmen doing business with the Japanese should be aware of the function and importance of the name-card and know how to use it. Because of its particular function, there is a prescribed manner for exchanging name-cards. The card should be presented while the very first stages of the introduction are taking place, so the Japanese recipient will be able to determine your position and rank and know how to respond to you.

The normal procedure is for the Japanese to hand you his name-card and accept yours at the same time, read your card, and then formally greet you—traditionally by bowing and making appropriate remarks. It is now also common for all parties to shake hands, as well as bow to each other. This process is naturally facilitated if one side of your name-card includes Japanese translations of your name, title, and company—and, of course, you should present your card "Japanese side up."

It is surprising how many foreign businessmen go to Japan or greet Japanese visitors in their own offices without having Japanese-language name-cards ready to pass out. It is not a matter of courtesy. It is a reflection of your business sense, your personal image of yourself and your company, your attitude toward Japan, and more.

Besides the role of the name-card itself often being misunderstood and misused by uninitiated foreign businessmen, the Western habit of immediately shaking hands upon meeting someone frequently messes up meetings with Japanese. The formal order is to exchange name-cards *before* bowing and shaking hands.

While not too serious, especially if the handshake is quickly followed up by the presentation of name-cards, this is an area where the foreign businessman *can* gain a few points by demonstrating his awareness and appreciation of Japanese customs.

As a result of Japan's "Vertical Society," rank pervades the lives of Japanese businessmen, wherever they may be. They joke among themselves that when they play golf, it is customary for them to tee off in accordance with their salaries (it used to be the capital of their companies).

In any meeting, the Japanese businessman is bound by the rules of the senior-junior ranking system and by the additional necessity of maintaining harmony. What he says, how he says it, and when he says it is determined by his rank within the group.

Another graphic indication of the attention paid to status is the common practice of making careful arrangements to seat individuals according to their rank at formal dinner parties and other official functions.

Habatsu
Behavior by the Numbers

For all of the cohesiveness and sameness exhibited by Japanese society when viewed from the outside, the Japanese are in fact splintered into big and little groups, economically, socially, and politically, with the various groups revolving around individual companies, government ministries, hospitals, schools, and sundry organizations. These thousands of separate groups are of vital importance because by opening or closing doors to individuals, they hold the keys to success for the overwhelming majority.

Success, for all except the rare individual in Japan, is getting into the "right" group. The individual can generally get into one of these choice vertically structured groups only at the bottom, when he or she is young and just out of school. The most conspicuous exceptions have traditionally been retiring high-level government bureaucrats who are regularly taken into industry at executive levels because of the value of the influence they retain with their former junior colleagues in their old bureaus. This practice is commonly referred to as *amakudari* (ah-mah-kuu-dah-ree) or "descending from heaven."

One implication of the word *amakudari* is that giving up the power, prestige, security, and harmony of a vice-minister's post for the rough uncertainty of the commercial world is a considerable step-down. Another implication, of course, is that such "heavenly beings" can do extraordinary things when it comes to dealing with their old ministries.

Another, new exception to the long-established custom of bringing in new employees or group members only at the bottom is called *chuto saiyo* (chuu-toe sie-yoe), which means "mid-career appointment." Beginning about 1970 it became expedient for many companies to go outside their "closed system" to occasionally hire middle-aged, experienced personnel with needed technical expertise—thus "mid-career" recruitment.

Not surprisingly, employees in the *chuto saiyo* category are generally not treated like "regular" employees. Their pay may be one or two steps below that being received by regular employees in their own age group (because to pay them the same would be "unfair" to the employees who had been with the company all their working lives), and they are often discriminated against by other employees in various subtle ways.

Despite the *amakudari* and *chuto saiyo* exceptions where major enterprises (but not government jobs) are concerned, most desirable companies are still basically closed to the entry of outsiders except by young people just out of school who come in at the bottom of the pyramid. Once an individual has become a member of a large company or elite organization and has spent several years there, it becomes either difficult or impossible for him to become a fully accepted member of another organization.

There are several reasons for this. In a system in which promotion, income, prestige, etc., are primarily based on seniority, a new member coming in anywhere except at the bottom (or the top) breaks the "chain" and may throw everyone directly below the new member off schedule for life, since there are only a specific number of upper-level managerial and executive slots.

When a Japanese quits a large company and moves to another one—something that is still very unusual—he cannot take his personal connections and good relations with him. Generally speaking, he will never to able to develop the same relationships over again with his new co-workers. Japanese managers who have switched employers and spent more than ten years with their new companies frequently report that they are still regarded as "outsiders."

Quitting a large, well-known company and going to another one—or being transferred by a parent company to a distant subsidiary or a young joint venture company—is therefore a serious proposition for a Japanese manager, because it means he has been cast adrift from the ties that mean the most to him.

Since both the grouping and advancement-by-seniority systems in Japan put everything on a personal basis, close human relations are the "cement" of Japanese society, in business as well as private life. One company will not do business with another company until the managers who would be involved in initiating and continuing the business have developed personal relations to the extent that they can satisfactorily *amaeru* with each other. This process of developing the necessary personal relations before establishing business ties with a new company is prescribed, meticulous, and time-consuming.

Gakubatsu
Rule by Cliques

As in all countries, Japan's institutions of higher learning are ranked, unofficially, by various standards—age, origin, size, wealth, reputation of the staff and facilities, their political and economic influence. Most important for the ambitious young man in Japan, they are also ranked on the basis of the career job opportunities almost completely reserved for graduates of the top universities.

In the early years of Japan's modernization, top government posts and choice managerial positions naturally went to graduates of the first universities—some of which were government-sponsored. As the years passed and other universities appeared, graduates of the oldest institutions continued to monopolize the best jobs in the country simply because they were favored by their alumni brothers who occupied top positions in most leading government ministries and companies.

This practice was inevitably categorized under the term *gakubatsu* (gah-kuu-baht-sue) or "school cliques." While informal, these cliques, each one pertaining to the graduates of a specific, elite university, continue to dominate top posts in government and in many commercial enterprises.

Tokyo Daigaku (Die-gah-kuu) or Tokyo University (Todai [Toe-die] for short) is at the apex of Japan's educational pyramid. Hundreds of young men and women impair their health and bring great mental suffering on themselves and their families each year in their attempts to pass the entrance examinations with a high enough score to get into Todai. Almost every year there are one or more students who commit suicide because of repeated failures to win admittance.

Japan's young know only too well that if they do not get into Todai they will probably be barred forever from several top-ranking companies and ministries because these institutions hire mostly Todai graduates. By the same token, those who succeed in getting into Tokyo University know they have it made the rest of their lives. It often seems, in fact, that it doesn't make too much difference whether they learn anything or not at Todai, just as long as they get in and graduate.

"The road to Todai begins in kindergarten," a Japanese saying goes as a way of describing how difficult it is for a student to get into the university. Competition is so fierce that by the early 1960s it had spread down to the kindergarten level—a certain number of them graduating more students who eventually succeeded in passing the entrance exams to Todai.

Japanese universities hold entrance examinations once a year. If a student taking the exam fails, in competition with all the other students taking the same examination, he or she has to wait a full year before trying to get into the same university again. High school graduates, who fail to get into the university of their choice and opt to wait until the following year to try again rather than take the examinations to a less desirable university, are popularly called *ronin* (roe-neen), literally "wave men," the old term for samurai warriors who lost their clan lord (for any reason) and roamed the country, often causing trouble.

In the case of Tokyo University, for every student who passes the entrance exams on the first attempt, several dozen fail and become *ronin*. Many who have gotten this far refuse to give up hope without a long struggle, and they go back year after year in the hope that they will make it the next time. Others, deciding that the odds against them are too great, give up and settle for a second- or third-choice university.

A similar situation exists, to a lesser degree, for several universities ranked immediately below Todai—Keio (Kay-oh), Waseda (Wah-say-dah), Kyoto University, Hitotsubashi (He-tote-sue-bah-she), Kobe University, etc. Like Todai, they enjoy the special "patronage" of certain enterprises and government bureaus.

The mystique of Todai is undergoing a metamorphosis, however, which will no doubt be welcomed by most Japanese. Its dominance of several of the leading ministries of the government and the upper echelons of management in many of the country's ranking companies continues, but there is increasing criticism of both the "arrogance" and the competence of Todai graduates, particularly in regard to the growth and profit positions some of the companies they head.

One Todai professor summed up the situation by saying that Todai graduates were intelligent but lacked imagination and the innovative spirit that was now needed by Japanese industry. He described the typical graduate as a "superior mediocrity."

At the same time, the criticism may also result in a change in the Todai approach to teaching and in the attitude of its graduates, refurbishing the tainted image of the famed university.

There is a special word used when referring to the "job-getting success" of graduates of specific high schools and universities: *shushokuritsu* (shuu-show-kuu-reet-sue), which means "the rate of employed versus the number of graduates." The percentage of graduates from a particular school who succeed in getting jobs with desirable companies or government ministries determines the school's *shushokuritsu*—the "job-getting success" of its students.

Sports activities are very popular and important in Japanese universities because leading companies like to hire well-known athletes. There is usually a club for each sport. Among club members, the *sempai-kohai* (senior-junior) syndrome reigns supreme, with emphasis on proper behavior of juniors toward seniors—behavior based on complete subordination. An alumnus *(sempai)* who is particularly outstanding for some reason is often referred to as *dai-sempai* or "great senior."

Occasionally, a *dai-sempai* who is a graduate of a particular university and is in a responsible position in a prestigious company will accept an invitation from his old sports club to visit its summer training camp. There, both school and club ties are reaffirmed, and it is made explicit that the *dai-sempai* will do all he can to help members of the club get into his company after they graduate.

Such relationships, established on a hot summer day on the playing field, are cherished for a lifetime by students who end up being employed by the company concerned, and they serve as a significant factor in major personnel decisions by leading Japanese companies.

Many of the elite universities set certain standards, such as the number of *A*'s an individual earns during the senior year, to determine whether or not the student gets a recommendation from his or her professor to a desirable company.

University students in their senior year also compete for the privilege of doing their theses under the direction of the most popular professors, who are often retained as consultants by leading enterprises and therefore have strong connections with the personnel departments of these companies. Each professor conducts a "thesis seminar" for fifteen to twenty students, helping them select topics and guiding them in their research and writing.

Western executives serving in Japan who are recognized authorities in certain business fields might benefit themselves and their firms by offering to act as free advisors to these "thesis seminars." By establishing such a relationship with universities, with individual professors and graduating students, the executives would come into contact with outstanding young men and women looking for career opportunities.

Nenbatsu
Up by the Year

Besides the *gakubatsu* or "school clique" factor in the headier heights of Japan's business and professional world, there are also *nenbatsu* or "year-clubs" in some ministries and many major corporations. A "year-club" is a grouping of all the new university graduates who entered the company or ministry the same year—regardless of what university they graduated from.

As members of a particular year-club accrue seniority in their organization they look out for each other. Their entry-year loyalty may be so strong they avoid developing close relationships with other co-workers, including those from the same university but from different graduating classes. Members of the same year-club expect to be promoted at the same time and thus move up the executive escalator together. Even when new employees do not formally align themselves in such clubs, they still form a close bond and they expect to go up in unison.

Some Japanese critics blame the year-clubs and advancement-by-seniority for an excess of assistant managers and managers in a typical Japanese company. But the larger and older the company, the deeper the systems are likely to be entrenched. The trend in the past has been for new companies and rapidly growing smaller companies to start out with a merit system, or at least a partial merit system, for pay and promotion purposes. But in all cases so far, the passing of time has seen the appearance—sometimes gradual and sometimes sudden—of the seniority system. The Japanese, say the country's businessmen-philosophers, like the security of it.

Because success in Japan is so intimately tied to educational level, as well as to the prestige of the university attended and because the highest ranking universities have been more or less sanctified as a result of their exalted role in the nation's life, the situation provides the foreigner with a way to get partially inside Japanese society. I say "partially" because no foreigner has ever entered all the way inside Japanese society and is not likely to in the foreseeable future.

This "way" consists of attending and graduating from one of the better-known and respected Japanese universities. Not only will the ties with your Japanese classmates approximate those among themselves, you are also accorded a certain amount of respect and acceptance by Japanese who graduated before you did, as well as by those who come after you. Attending school together in Japan is very much like becoming a blood brother in the American Indian sense.

Shudan Ishiki
All Together Now

Most top Japanese businessmen tend to be businessmen-philosophers, very much concerned with the ethics and morality of the Japanese enterprise system and its perpetuation. One of the ways they attempt to achieve their purpose is to promote a type of group thinking called *shudan ishiki* (shuu-dahn ee-she-kee). This way of thinking emphasizes the functions and goals of the group, as opposed to thinking in terms of experience, qualifications, and responsibilities of the individual.

The *shudan ishiki* type of thinking has, of course, long been an ideal of Japanese society.

3

Wa
Peace and Harmony
in an Up-Down World

Shinto
The Way of the Gods

No society, whatever its structure, can remain viable very long without explicit rules and restrictions governing the behavior of its members. For Japan's "Vertical Society," these guidelines were based on principles incorporated in, among others, the words *wa* (wah), *on* (own), *giri* (ghee-ree), *ninjo* (neen-joe), and *tsukiai* (t'sue-key-aye).

Wa, which may be translated as "peace and harmony," is one of the most important words in the vocabulary of Japan. The Japanese concept of peace and tranquility (in behavior as well as in thought) is implicit in the concept of *amae*, or indulgent love, described earlier, and may have originated in Shinto, the native religion.

Shinto (Sheen-toe), the Way of the Gods, is an ancient body of beliefs, without a bible or other written work, which tells the Japanese that they are the descendants of a group of heavenly beings, that all men and all things are spiritual brothers, that both spiritual and physical harmony are necessary to keep man and things right with the cosmos.

The Shinto concept that is most explicit in Japan's management philosophy is belief in *musubi* (muu-sue-bee), or "the

36

undifferentiated coexistence of men, nature, and the gods." Translated into practical terms, Japanese businessmen believe that spiritual unity should be the foundation for all relations between management and employees.

The Way of the Gods teaches that every man is his brother's keeper and that to achieve and practice *amae* all men must be selfless. Of course, there were contradictions in the social structure of the Japanese right from the very beginning, with those descended from "superior deities" becoming superior beings, but in the main, Shintoism resulted in the majority of the Japanese, until modern times, being strongly influenced by the concept of "instinctive unselfishness" and harmonious behavior.

In any event, the concept of *wa* has been repeatedly designated throughout Japan's history as the foundation of the country's Imperial system and the ideal for which all Japanese should strive. Still today, the word *wa* is forever on the tongues of politicians, statesmen, and businessmen alike as they exhort their fellow countrymen to control themselves and to set an example for the world. There is in fact an old Japanese belief that they were divinely ordained to spread Japanese *wa* to the rest of the world (not unlike the obsession of Western missionaries to spread Christianity to all people).

Buddhism
The Way of the Bamboo

Much of the passivity and "bending with the bamboo" associated with Japanese manners and attitudes is attributed to Buddhism, which was introduced into Japan from China in the sixth century A.D., and has since coexisted with Shintoism as well as various aspects of Confucianism.

While there are many facets of Buddhism, a basic tenet is coexistence of man and nature, and nonviolence. The practicalities of life, however, led the Japanese to develop such concepts as passive resistance to get one's way, "losing to win," and jujitsu, the martial art that turns an opponent's strength and aggressiveness into a weapon against him.

Confucianism, the third religious ethic that played a vital

role in the shaping and coloring of Japanese culture, was primarily responsible for the philosophy of loyalty to one's superiors that justified and controlled the superior-subordinate vertical structure of the society.

On
The Web That Binds

Within the context of the traditional Japanese social system and its emphasis on *wa*, the key word was *on* (own), which refers to the various obligations—to themselves, to each other, to their clan or country, and to the world—that all Japanese are automatically "assigned" at birth, or that they incurred during their lifetime.

These various obligations, all designed to maintain peace and harmony within the confines of the superior-inferior vertical system, formed the principles on which Japan's extraordinary society grew—a society that was built upon a class and ranking system in which position, severely prescribed manners, rights, and responsibilities were absolute values that were imposed upon the people with relentless power.

As long as they remained members of their society, the Japanese of preindustrial Japan were not free to say anything, take any action, in fact have any thought that was not prescribed by the dictates of their position and by the *on* adhering to that position. A Japanese could not (and still cannot!) even say "sit down" without using words that properly denoted his position in life in relation to the person addressed. In bowing, a Japanese had to know not only when to bow but also how low to bow, how long the bow should be maintained, and how many times to bow.

Saho
Etiquette as Virtue

It is difficult for the Western mind to grasp just how important these manners were to early Japanese. Westerners are generally conditioned to conduct their lives according to certain abstract principles, with manners playing only a minor role. In Japan, the emphasis was reversed and a social system was forged in which the ultimate virtue was a prescribed conduct. Morality, as it is known in the West, was an aspect of manners.

From around the sixth century A.D. to the beginning of the modern era in 1868, the Japanese were more concerned with form than sincerity or accomplishment. The people were required to walk a certain way, to move their hands a certain way, to open doors a certain way, to sleep with their head pointing in a certain direction and with their legs arranged a certain way. The style and manner of their dress was prescribed by law for several generations before the beginning of the modern era. Their manner of eating was severely prescribed; they could enter a house only a certain way and greet each other only a certain way. Even physical movements necessary to perform many types of work were definitively established and no deviation was allowed.

So rigid and so severe were these prescribed manners that they long ago became a part of the Japanese personality, permeating and shaping every phase and facet of their lives, and were passed on from one generation to the next. Today most foreign businessmen dealing with Japan quickly learn that there is still a "Japanese way" to do everything as a result of this meticulous conditioning over the centuries.

Japan's Feudal Age was full of amazing and sometimes shocking incidents of what happened to people who behaved in an other than expected manner. One of the most recounted of these incidents involves a farmer named Sogo who went over the head of his local lord to complain about starvation taxes to the Shogun, Japan's military dictator. For having broken a rule of conduct, Sogo was forced to watch his three small sons beheaded. Then he and his wife were crucified— although his complaint proved justified and the local lord was later removed from office.

Japanese society was therefore utterly cruel in that a man's morals were *visible for all to see.* For many centuries, a serious breach of etiquette in Japan was just as much a crime as murder or robbery was in the West. And the broken rule of conduct that made the death penalty inevitable did not have to be very important from our point of view.

Until well after the middle of the nineteenth century, it was legal for a samurai, the sword-carrying, privileged ruling class of Japan, to immediately kill any common individual who failed to show him proper respect—and a disproportionate number of the samurai were among the most arrogant and status-conscious men that ever lived.

Perhaps worse than this was the fact that whenever a Japanese failed to live up to his obligations or was remiss in his manners toward anyone of importance, he lost his place in life. This, still today, is an important consideration in the lives of most Japanese.

Not only class, but also sex, age, family ties, and previous dealings determined the behavior of the Japanese in every area of their lives. Form and manner, the outward expressions of the system, were sanctified as virtues. The extent to which this stratified and categorized society developed in Japan would be unbelievable if it were not for the fact that it still flourishes today, especially in the professional and business world, in only a slightly diluted form.

Business, as well as other relations, in Japan have traditionally been conducted within the web of this etiquette system, based on personal obligations owed to others. All dealings, public and private, were (and still are to a great extent) conducted within a set of rules that were designed to prevent trouble, to prevent or control change. Japan's "Golden Rule" was perfect hierarchical harmony at any human cost!

It was the law for many generations that in case of quarrels or fights among the people, both sides would be equally punished without inquiry into the cause of the fight and regardless of whether one party was completely innocent. This discouraged public squabbles of any kind among the people, and it so deeply embedded the habit of public harmony in the Japanese that until about 1950, one could live in Japan for many years without ever seeing or hearing a public row.

If someone stepped on another's toes or had an accident, the persons involved bowed to each other, mumbled a series of polite expressions, and went on their way; or they very quietly exchanged name-cards if the accident was serious. Even taxi drivers adhered to this rigid principle of formal politeness until as late as the mid-1950s. People seldom raised their voices in anger and it was even rarer for one person to strike another in public.

In order to guarantee conformity to such strict rules, it was necessary for Japan's feudal government to make use of an Orwellian system of control and punishment. Like the inhabitants of George Orwell's *1984,* but predating it by several centuries, the Japanese of feudal Japan were supposed to watch their families, friends, and neighbors and report all infractions of the rules to the proper authorities—often with disastrous results for those reported.

The control system in Japan was in fact more encompassing and more cruelly enforced than Orwell's futuristic nightmare. At least in Orwell's world it was kept on an individual basis, but in Japan the feudal authorities held a man's family and sometimes his neighbors or even his whole village responsible for his actions. If he broke a regulation, the whole group was liable for punishment. Instances in which an entire family was destroyed or a clan broken up for the transgressions of one person are a compelling part of Japanese history.

Today, the businessman in Japan reflects the results of these centuries of conditioning in harmony in many ways: his dread of personal responsibility; his preference for mutual cooperation and group effort; his tendency to follow the mass and to imitate success; his reluctance to oppose anyone openly; his desire to submerge his individualism into his surroundings, etc. As a result of his conditioning, he is and has been for over a thousand years the nearly perfect Organization Man.

A further result of the enforcement of Japan's Golden Rule of *wa,* and a factor that makes it possible to generalize about Japanese businessmen with an astonishing degree of accuracy, is their mental homogeneity. As early as the tenth century, Japanese society had already developed into a highly specialized, intense, and uniform civilization in which the people dressed the same within their class, ate the same foods, were subjected to the same experiences, had the same stock of knowledge and the same prejudices.

This sameness was so pervasive that, according to cultural historians, ordinary means of communication were unnecessary. The Japanese were so attuned to one another's attitudes and manners that the slightest hint or gesture was sufficient to convey their meaning with an almost magical facility.

It is not hard to understand the reasons for this extraordinary similarity of the Japanese. First, there was nearly complete isolation from the rest of the world for the first several thousand years of the country's human history. Second, the small land area of the islands resulted in all the various influences that shaped the culture being felt at about the same time and more or less evenly by all the people.

Jesse F. Steiner, describing Japan before the Pacific War in his book *Behind the Japanese Mask* (Macmillan, New York, 1943), was more matter-of-fact in his analysis of the homogeneity of the Japanese. He pointed out that the Japanese should be easy to understand because their lives for centuries had been governed by stereotyped conventions and a rigid social code. There was, he noted, an appropriate behavior for every situation and a prescribed form to follow for every action of life, both public and private.

Giri
The Personal Code

While *on* may be said to be the "universal" obligation the Japanese accrue as a result of being born, raised, educated, and employed, *giri* (ghee-ree) is the personal code, the deep sense of duty, of honor, that compels them to fulfill their obligations—for good or bad.

Both *on* and *giri* are reciprocal in nature and derive from a relationship in which the subordinate is expected to extend service and loyalty to the superior, and the superior is obligated to demonstrate responsibility and gratitude to the subordinate. Without *giri* the *on* system would disintegrate.

This code of honor of the Japanese is often referred to as "*giri* to one's name." Failure to keep *giri* to one's name results in loss of *face*. Westerners are of course familiar with the idea of "losing face" because the term has been applied to Japanese and other Asians. The words and the idea have been bandied about since the turn of the twentieth century. But few appreciate the significance of the term or how important the idea of *face* is to everyday business and social life in Japan. To lose face means much more to a Japanese than simply being embarrassed or insulted, except in the very strongest sense of the words.

Although such great sensitivity to all outside influences is a tremendous handicap for the Japanese, it is not something they can take off like a coat. It is part of their national character. It is especially important for people who have professional status of any kind or degree to protect their face. Maintaining their face or reputation as a professional person does not mean, however, that they have to be skilled in their line of work or conduct themselves ethically. It means, instead, that they cannot, in *giri* to their name, admit ignorance or inability or allow anyone to besmirch their name without serious consequences to their self-image and sense of well-being.

Ninjo
Human Feelings Come First

Giri without human guidelines would have been unthinkable for the Japanese. These were provided by other principles within the framework of appropriate *ninjo* (neen-joe), or human feelings. One of the first things even the casual observer in Japan learns is that the Japanese measure, or try to measure, everything in terms of "human feelings." Their business system, they say, respects human feelings—while most foreign business systems do not.

In short, it is typical Japanese ethics and behavior to give precedence to human feelings in most situations where possible, including many occasions when objective-thinking Western businessmen would unhesitatingly give precedence to profit considerations or other such "nonhuman" factors.

Many of the aspects of doing business in Japan that baffle and frustrate Western businessmen can only be understood in terms of *ninjo*.

Along with their dislike of "cold" logic, the Japanese are inclined to be suspicious of anyone who is a smooth talker or who talks fast. They are especially turned off by someone who talks "too much." On the other hand, being a "good talker" is cultivated in the United States and is prized as a major business asset. Thus when Japanese and American businessmen and politicians meet, there is often a serious clash.

American businessmen who are inexperienced or insensitive to cultural differences often attempt to overcome communication problems with the Japanese by talking more than usual, repeating themselves, and more often than not, raising their voices. In the Japanese context of things, it is better to say too little than too much, even though it may take much longer to arrive at an understanding.

Kao Wo Tateru
"Save My Face!"

Most "old-fashioned" Japanese businessmen still believe it is the height of rudeness to come out in the open and state opinions or unpleasant truths frankly because there is the possibility of loss of face. Whereas Americans, especially, are in the habit of "laying all their cards on the table," the Japanese have been conditioned to speak vaguely, and when necessary to resort to circumlocutions rather than make a frank statement that might give offense.

This basic difference in attitudes and manners puts both Japanese and Westerners at a disadvantage when they are dealing with each other. The Western businessman too often assumes that his openness is being reciprocated, and it may be too late to rectify matters when he discovers his mistake.

Japanese companies have a particularly sensitive "face" that must be maintained. In premodern days, this concept was often expressed by using the term *noren* (no-rain), which in its original meaning refers to the short, split curtains the Japanese have been hanging across the doors of shops and restaurants for centuries. The *noren* are usually made of navy blue cotton and bear the name or crest of the owner. In the early days *noren* came to embody the "face" of the business concerned, and business owners zealously guarded their symbols from being misused or abused.

Eventually it became customary for the owners of established *noren* to allow favored or ranking employees to go out and set up their own businesses, under the *noren* of their former employers, thus becoming branches or subsidiaries or "related" firms. In this way, a number of businesses gradually formed a network of closely affiliated companies spread throughout the country.

Many of the *noren* famous in Japan today go back several hundred years and in some cases the owners of famous ones lease them out. The well-known Fuji Bank does business under the *noren* of the Yasuda family, one of Japan's largest and most respected *zaibatsu* (zie-baht-sue). Present-day businessmen value their company face just as highly as their predecessors did.

It is common—especially in Osaka—to hear a businessman say he will not or cannot do something because of respect he must pay to his "face" or because it might scar his company's face. Still, the Japanese are always being forced to put their face on the line for one reason or another; therefore, they frequently use the phrase, *Kao wo tatette kudasai,* or "Please save my face!"

Tsukiai
Paying Social Debts

The Japanese are naturally sensitive to incurring new obligations arbitrarily because there are so many they can't avoid and because discharging their normal obligations is such a heavy burden. Honoring the obligations that develop between individuals who have a special relationship—not always a happy or pleasant duty—is more often than not done simply to maintain friendly relations for the sake of *tsukiai* (t'sue-key-aye), as the Japanese so commonly say.

In practical terms, *tsukiai* refers to the social debt the student owes his professor, the employee owes his employer, the politician owes his patron, or that anybody owes to anyone who does him or her a favor, especially of a vital nature whose effects are continuous over an extended period of time. To owe *tsukiai* and to have someone owe you *tsukiai* in Japan is an important social and economic factor.

All Japanese are under strong pressure to honor their *tsu-kiai* debts. Failure to do so is a serious transgression if the occasion is an appropriate one, such as when a professor seeks a favor from a former student who now occupies a high position in some company or government office.

Shokaijo
A Shortcut to Success

In business the *tsukiai* factor is often used in the form of a *shokaijo* (show-kie-joe), or "introduction," a very important ingredient in Japanese etiquette and ethics in business.

Westerners are familiar with the practice of giving and receiving introductions in the regular conduct of their businesses. But the system used in the United States, for example, does not compare with the role the *shokaijo* play in Japan. Americans are not compelled by generations of conditioning and centuries of tradition to treat an introduction as anything more than mere politeness. The American businessman on the receiving end of a *shokaijo* can turn the caller away or decline to take any action on his behalf without fearing that his relationship with the man who gave the introduction will suffer. Not so the Japanese, particularly if the introduction is from a valued friend, a superior, or an important business contact. The businessman who is most susceptible to an introduction is the man most concerned with maintaining his "face" among those to whom he owes *tsukiai*.

The *shokaijo* itself is institutionalized in Japan with wide ramifications that touch on many aspects of daily life. It owes its role and power to several cultural influences: the exclusivity and wariness toward outsiders that is inherent in the vertically structured group system, the desire of the Japanese not to lose face for any reason, the principle of group responsibility, and their tendency to avoid personal involvement with outsiders or strangers.

The least that can be said is that in Japan it is considered rude to approach a person or a company directly without an introduction from a mutual friend or business contact. If you go through proper channels—that is, the *shokaijo*—some of the responsibility shifts to the third party and provides an element of security. The Japanese tend to be suspicious of anyone who approaches them without an introduction, and most Japanese would not think of making such an approach themselves in dealing with other Japanese.

There are several types of *shokaijo* commonly used by the Japanese when they want to meet someone for business purposes. The most common one is from someone to whom the person you want to meet is personally obligated, such as one of his superiors, an old university professor, someone who has helped his family, or a close relative or personal friend. Another popular type of introduction is one from a senior executive in a company with which the person you want to meet has substantial business obligations, such as from the vice-president of the bank where he has made a loan or from some important buyer or supplier.

Less effective but still useful is an introduction from a senior officer in a company with which the individual's company has business relations. A nonpersonal introduction from a well-known bank, company, or other organization is probably the weakest of the introductions but is better than none. The foreign executive who plans on doing business in Japan or is already in business there certainly should make an effort to obtain introductions to any individual or company he wants to approach.

While the best introduction is often a personal one to an individual, the foreign businessman will generally find that he cannot rely *only* on an approach to a single individual in a Japanese company. To be successful, any approach must also take into consideration all other sections and departments concerned.

Again, while there is only one "right" way to meet a Japanese businessman, which is through an introduction, the Japanese regularly make exceptions to this where foreigners are concerned. In fact, foreigners who show up at Japanese companies without having either appointments or introductions may be shown into the office of the highest executive available. This, however, is usually no more than "Japanese politeness" and cannot be taken as a sign of interest in the caller or his purpose.

Knowing the *shokaijo* system exists and knowing how to use it leads many individuals in Japan to specialize in taking unethical or unappreciated advantage of it. Some people make a business of "selling" their status by giving introductions to persons and accepting gifts and other favors in return. In particular, advertising-space salesmen are notorious for taking advantage of the power of the *shokaijo*. These salesmen somehow get closer to a businessman or well-known, respected and influential figure—the higher and the more important the better—and ask him to write a few words of introduction on several of his name-cards. The introduction usually consists of only a few words, like "This is Mr. So-and-So. Please do what you can for him."

The salesmen then take the cards to the businessman's circle of friends in other companies and sell advertising space to them. There is often little or no talk about advertising as such. The salesmen are more likely to say that their publication would like to have the "support" of the company. By this time the man on the other end of the *shokaijo* knows exactly what is going on and, more often than not, will sign the advertising contract or in some cases hand over the amount of money suggested by the salesman. Most companies in Japan have a special fund set aside, called *tsukiai-ryo*, or "social debt funds," to pay off such "debts."

It should be emphasized, however, that the businessman who is put in a position in which he feels obligated to pay out *tsukiai-ryo* may consider that he is being "taken" and may resent it strongly.

Hoshonin
The Guarantor

The use of the *shokaijo*, a deep-rooted social and business custom in Japan, derives its power from the practical and psychological need of the Japanese to have some kind of "guarantee" before they can bring themselves to become involved with someone with whom they do not have an *amae* relationship. Besides the *shokaijo* itself, this need for guarantees led to the development of another institutionalized function and figure in Japanese society, namely the *hoshonin* (hoe-sho-neen) or "guarantor."

In numerous instances involving official documents, establishing credit, and so on, the Japanese system requires a *hoshonin* who accepts responsibility for the individual's character, trustworthiness, and behavior. On a higher level, the person who gives a *shokaijo* becomes partly and sometimes wholly responsible for whatever may come of it—both the good and the bad. A *hoshonin,* by comparison, accepts full responsibility both in principle and in fact.

There are many cases of an introduction from one Japanese to another apparently having no more significance than the somewhat casual letter or note of introduction common in the West, in which nothing more complicated or compelling than simple courtesy is involved. But favors that are small and completely insignificant from the Western viewpoint are not bestowed lightly in Japan, especially when they occur through an introduction.

Chukai-Sha
The In-between Man

The ultimate in the *shokaijo* concept in Japan is the *chukai-sha* (chuu-kie-shah), or a person who acts as a go-between in business affairs. Of course, the concept and role of the go-between or intermediary is familiar in the West, but again, the Japanese have institutionalized the function, and it plays a much greater role there. The *chukai-sha* in business and the *nakodo* (nah-koe-doe) in arranged marriages play a much greater and more important role in life in Japan.

The advantages of using a *chukai-sha* in business are numerous and not really mysterious. In the first place, the better go-betweens have a wide circle of friends and connections and are respected and trusted individuals. In Japan, where face-to-face communication by strangers is very difficult, the go-between can carry on most of the dialogue, help each side avoid losing face, and eventually smooth the way for the development of a formal relationship between the two parties if their interests merge.

The *chukai-sha* can be especially helpful to the foreign businessman in Japan, providing invaluable counsel on what to
do and what not to do to maintain peace and harmony and
negotiate successfully with Japanese companies. Recognizing
this, some foreign companies operating in Japan have had
chukai-sha on retainer for years.

O'miyage
Giving to the Cause

Another important aspect of maintaining good relations,
keeping *wa*, and getting things done in Japan comes under the
general heading of gift-giving. There are, broadly speaking,
three categories of gift-giving in Japan. On the lowest order
are the *te-miyage* (tay-me-yah-gay) or "hand gifts" given to the
host when you are invited to someone's home or to someone
who does you a favor while you are traveling. Gifts given
when making home visits are likely to consist of cakes, pas-
tries, boxes of fruit, or traditional Japanese food delicacies. (It
is not the custom for the host to open these gifts while the
guest is present.)

The second category of gifts is of those given in midsummer and at the end of the year. The midsummer gift-giving
occasion is called *Chugen* (chuu-gain); the year-end gift-giving
season is known as *Seibo* (say-e-boe). The end of the year is the
most important gift-giving season in Japan, because this is
when virtually all companies give gifts to their clients and
customers.

Companies, in fact, are the biggest gift-givers in Japan.
They give year-end gifts to "reward" customers for past patronage, to express gratitude, and to build up obligation for
future business, etc. During the years that I had monthly
printing done by Dai-Nippon (die-neep-pone), Japan's largest printing company, the department in charge of my account had a case of beer or some other useful commodity
delivered to my home every year just before New Year's.
Being one of the largest printing companies in the world,
with thousands of customers, one can imagine the size of Dai-
Nippon's annual year-end gift bill.

On an individual basis, subordinates give gifts to superiors, and people in general present gifts to *onjin* (own-jeen) or "benefactors" to whom they are obligated for past favors.

Most Japanese businessmen who go abroad take gifts of varying value to give to people they meet. For casual gifts to people who show them some hospitality, the visitors usually give relatively inexpensive gifts that are representative of Japan, such as folding fans, carved *kokeshi* (koe-kay-she) dolls, miniature calculators, etc. For important, established or potential business associates, the gifts are often fairly expensive and elaborate.

Because such gift-giving is institutionalized, the Japanese are naturally pleased when their foreign guests or business counterparts follow the custom. A set of golf clubs or a case of good Scotch is probably more appreciated in Japan than in any other country.

The third category of gift-giving in Japan comes under the heading of *o'tsukaimono* (oh-t'sue-kie-moe-no), "something to be used," and is practiced throughout the year on every social and economic level. An *o'tsukaimono* gift is specifically given to a person when you are seeking a favor from that person. Rather than regard the gift as a form of bribery, the Japanese feel that it is rude to ask a favor of someone without giving them something in return.

Gift-giving on an elaborate scale is not a recent development in Japan. Like so many other things, it has its roots deep in the culture, and in earlier times it was as meticulously hedged in by rules as other areas of Japanese life. There were, in fact, specific rules prescribing exactly what item or thing was appropriate to give to people on particular occasions and according to their social rank. It was also prescribed as to how such gifts should be wrapped, using what materials in what manner. And finally, the procedure for presenting gifts to important superior-ranking persons was minutely detailed.

The importance attached to the proper choice, wrapping, and presentation of gifts is apparent from the fact that well-to-do families often had one member whose primary responsibility was to know and advise the household on gift-giving protocol.

Moshiwake Arimasen
Apology without End

With so many areas of life so meticulously prescribed, it was virtually impossible for the Japanese of feudal Japan to avoid transgressions against their highly refined and aggressively enforced etiquette system. To compensate for the bonds their manners imposed on them, and to help prevent the system from breaking down under its own weight, the Japanese gave great power to the apology. Most minor and many major transgressions against the system could be wiped clean by admission of guilt, and apology, and a demonstration of humility and regret.

An apologetic, humble attitude, especially by public figures, is still considered an essential virtue by the Japanese. In fact, for the Japanese to function smoothly within the web of their social obligations, it is necessary to learn very early how and when to humiliate themselves, to apologize humbly. There are so many ways in which the Japanese can give or take offense that the apology is also an institutionalized practice. The Japanese apologize for real as well as "pretended" shortcomings as often as Americans brag about their imagined ability and learning. The purpose of the Japanese apology is to avoid ill will, friction, or anything else that might rub supersensitive people the wrong way.

The apology expressed by the term *sumimasen* (sue-me-mah-sin)—literally, "it [the guilt I feel] is without end"—is the most common word for saying "I'm sorry" where small transgressions are concerned. *Moshiwake arimasen* (Moe-she-wah-kay ah-ree-mah-sin)—"I have no excuse" (and submit myself to your mercy)—is used in more serious situations. These terms, expressed several times amidst much bowing and facial signs of humility and regret, are often followed by *O'yurushi kudasai* (Oh-yuu-rue-she kuu-dah-sie), "Please forgive me."

Within the context of the Japanese system, the greatest sin is to be guilty of a crime, of any kind, and refuse to admit or express regret over it. Thus exceptional importance is attached to the apology.

For a Japanese (also for Koreans and Chinese) to confess to

a transgression, apologize, and express sincere regret is more or less the same in the Western sense as a guilty person being punished and rehabilitated at the same time. If the admission and apology are sincere, the Japanese forgive completely (rather than demand long-term punishment as is the case in the West).

Ojigi
Politeness Makes Perfect

The first-time visitor to Japan is always struck by the wonderful politeness of the people. No other Japanese trait or accomplishment has received so much praise. But there is an element of misunderstanding inherent in accepting this politeness at face value because it often misleads Westerners who are unfamiliar with the character and role of traditional Japanese etiquette.

For one thing, not all of the famous politeness of the Japanese should automatically be equated with feelings of kindness, regard, or respect for others—a reaction that is all too common where first-time visitors to Japan are concerned. The Japanese are, of course, perfectly capable of being polite in the fullest sense of the word and probably are genuinely more polite than most other people, but what the foreigner sees, and is often overly impressed by, is strictly a mechanical role that has little or nothing to do with the personal feelings of the individuals involved.

Many Westerners, especially American tourists, lavish praise upon the Japanese for this formal politeness. But most are basing their judgment of Japanese politeness on such things as the pretty, doll-like elevator and escalator girls who work in department stores and deluxe hotels. These girls, picked for looks and dressed in cute uniforms, stand and bow and repeat the same lines all day long in self-effacing, heart-rending voices that remind one of the chirping of baby birds that have fallen out of their nest.

The *ojigi* (oh-jee-ghee) or "bow" is the most visible manifestation of Japan's traditional etiquette. It is used for both greetings and farewells, when expressing appreciation or thanks, when apologizing, when asking an important favor—and when requesting any kind of action from a government bureaucrat.

The occasion and the parties involved in an *ojigi* determine the kind of bow that is appropriate. The lower the bow and the longer one holds the position, the stronger is the indication of respect, gratitude, sincerity, obeisance, humility, contriteness, etc.

Generally speaking, there are three kinds or degrees of bowing: the informal bow, the formal bow, and the *saikeirei* (sie-kay-ee-ray-e) or "highest form of salutation." In the light, informal bow, the body is bent at approximately a fifteen-degree angle with the hands at the sides. This bow is used for all casual occasions between people of all rank.

The formal bow requires that the body be bent to about thirty degrees, with the hands close together, palms down, on the knees. Ordinarily the bower holds this pose for only two or three seconds, then automatically returns to the upright position. If the other party remains bowed for a longer period, it is polite for the recipient to bow again. The recipient is often the superior who will generally respond to a formal bow with a fifteen-degree bow. The other party may bow a second and a third time. Synchronizing the bows so that both parties rise at approximately the same time can be tricky, and sometimes is unintentionally embarrassing.

When one party wants to emphasize the salutation and holds the pose for an unusually long period of time—while intoning appropriate remarks—the recipient must continue to make short bows, usually of gradually lessening degrees, to properly acknowledge the other bower's action.

The slow, deep *saikeirei* bow, which was the bow used to members of the Imperial family and Shogunate in earlier days, is only occasionally used now, generally by elder people who have a tendency to go back to the old ways as they grow older.

Businessmen who go to *ryokan* (rio-khan) inns or geisha houses may be greeted by maids or geisha who bow to them while sitting on the floor. It is not expected that one get down on the floor to return such bows—but it can be the beginning of a lot of fun!

The Japanese reputation for politeness breaks down very easily and quickly in many situations, particularly in those involving government offices, and often in business contexts as well. I have often gone into business offices in which there were dozens of people and had to go to extreme lengths to get someone to acknowledge my presence. At first I thought this peculiar reaction was brought on by the fact that I was a foreigner. Since the Japanese usually never expect a foreigner to speak their language, I was prepared to believe that they hesitated to say anything because no one could speak English or that they were simply bashful. It soon became obvious, however, that Japanese visitors were also regularly subjected to the same treatment, particularly in government offices.

Further observation and experience taught me how to shorten the waiting period—at least in business offices—but direct action on my part was still required. This consisted of catching the eye of anyone in the office who glanced up at me, then bowing very rapidly before he or she could turn away. The most effective bow to use in this situation, it seems, is a short, jerky one. This action triggers a reflex in the Japanese, and the party bows back, thus acknowledging your presence. He or she is then strongly obligated to follow up this step by coming to you or sending someone to find out what you want.

The problem of making the initial contact in a typical Japanese office is complicated by the fact that the office generally does not have a reception area or a receptionist or anyone responsible for greeting visitors. There may be a long counter running down the side of the office, but no one "man's" the counter. Usually when you go from a hallway into an office, you are confronted by rows of desks, with none of them positioned toward the entrance.

Another element in Japanese politeness (outside of unexpected visits to business offices) is the compulsion most Japanese have to make sure every foreign visitor, whether businessman or tourist, has a good time and leaves with a good impression of the country and its people. As a result of this compulsion, the Japanese are rightfully famous for their hospitality, and visitors who are not used to this kind of royal treatment are often overwhelmed by it.

The main point for the foreign businessman to keep in mind is that he should not confuse the politeness or hospitality of the Japanese with either weakness on their part or strength on his part. If he is really being courted by the Japanese, he may have to eventually limit the amount of hospitality he accepts to avoid being put at a serious disadvantage, physically as well as psychologically. Most Japanese businessmen are conditioned to regular drinking bouts. They also regularly bargain as a group. The lone visitor who goes into a bargaining session with a Japanese team after several nights on the town has his work cut out for him.

Kyoso
Competition by the Numbers

Before the modern era in Japan, most personal competition, especially within groups, was taboo because it resulted in friction and disharmony—the opposite of *wa*. In fact, the Japanese were taught that competition for personal, selfish purposes was criminal. The Japanese did not have a word for competition until one was deliberately coined by educator Yukichi Fukuzawa, the founder of Keio University, in the latter part of the 1800s.

While there are now many areas and ways in which the Japanese compete against each other fiercely, especially in education, the Japanese business system in general has maintained the old sanctions against individual competition, and it continues to promote the concept and practice of group action and team spirit.

There are other cultural factors involved in the taboos against personal competition among the Japanese. One of the worst things that can befall any Japanese is to be shamed and made to lose "face." Personal competition, with a few sanctioned exceptions such as in athletic contests, always carries with it the danger of being shamed. The foreign businessman should always remember that his contacts in Japanese companies, regardless of their rank, are not "officially" in competition with their colleagues, and they will resist any attitude or behavior that might make them appear to be competing against their own co-workers.

There have been and still are numerous occasions when the foreign businessman says, in effect, to a Japanese contact, "Look! You cooperate with me and help me get this deal through, and it will make you a big man in your company!" The one thing that would inevitably make it impossible for a Japanese to reach the higher or highest echelons of his company would be for him to break step with his co-workers or to strike out on his own.

Even though the Japanese are imbued with a compulsion to better themselves, to rise to the same level as those who are higher, and even though this compulsion is one of the prime forces motivating the Japanese economy, the extraordinary drive this gives the Japanese must generally be channeled into group effort within the framework of the Japanese company system.

Jicho
Staying out of Trouble

Another distinctive feature of Japanese life that is designed to promote *wa* and help the individual maintain essential dignity is expressed in the word *jicho* (jee-choe), which means "to respect one's self," to be prudent.

As is so often the case, however, respecting one's self in the Japanese context is not exactly the same as within Western cultures. Practicing *jicho* means to do nothing that would result in criticism and lessen one's chances for success. It means to be exquisitely wary of getting involved in anything that might make one stand out from the crowd and become subject to criticism.

The need to avoid criticism, of course, has a profound effect on the options and behavior of employees and managers in Japanese companies.

4

Kaisha
The Japanese Company

Uchi-No Kaisha
Companies as "Family Clans"

In Japanese, the word for company, *kaisha* (kie-shah), has strong connotations of "community." In referring to their place of employment, the Japanse typically use the term *uchi* (uu-chee), which means "inside" or "my house," in a possessive sense—*uchi-no kaisha* or "my company." This means a lot more than "the place where I work."

For those Japanese who work for large, well-known companies, the place where they work, *shokuba* (show-kuu-bah), takes precedence over their profession or the kind of work they do. When asked what they do for a living, the Japanese generally will not say they are teachers, engineers, carpenters, salesmen, or whatever. They will say they are members of the staff of Chiyoda High School, of Sanyo Electric Company, of Takenaka Construction Company, or of Nissan Motors. Profession, *shokugyo* (show-kuu-g'yoe), takes a back seat to *shokuba* (place of work).

The extent to which the Japanese identify with their employers is generally so strong it prevents them from having or developing any interests or links with others in their profession. In many professions, members of different organizations do, in fact, avoid communicating with each other.

In the United States, two people in any work category can

58

often establish a deep and satisfying rapport within minutes of their first meeting, even under the most casual or incidental circumstances. Such relationships can be especially deep and satisfying if the two happen to be in the same profession, whether they are truck drivers, bakers, or doctors. In Japan, such spontaneous horizontal relationships are practically out of the question.

The fact that the loyalty of the individual Japanese worker or manager is almost totally absorbed by his own seniority-ranked group makes it difficult for him to establish close relationships with any outsider, including those who are in the same line of work. On the contrary, there is a special feeling of wariness and sometimes hostility between Japanese and their professional counterparts within as well as outside their own companies.

The exclusivity inherent in the vertically ranked company system in Japan is so powerful that is makes it difficult, and sometimes impossible, for a group or a company to do business with another group or firm with which it does not have "established relations." When a company for some unavoidable reason is forced to engage in a business transaction with someone or some organization without close, personal ties having already been established, they refer to it as "doing business with the enemy."

This taboo is so deeply ingrained it sometimes leads to absolutely ludicrous situations, such as a company failing to act on a vital piece of information simply because it did not come from someone with whom the company has "personal relations."

Another business practice that seems especially strange to the foreign businessman is that in Japan the most capable or hardest working employee is not always the most likely to be promoted. The seniority system notwithstanding, the rank-and-file Japanese do not like for professionally superior people to be promoted faster than they are. They are afraid the promoted person will be more concerned about him or herself than about fellow workers. The Japanese way is to promote the person who gets along with everybody, is good at maintaining harmony, is flexible, and can be expected to be concerned about the welfare of all.

Recognition and advancement in Japanese companies do not depend so much on ability or achievement as upon length of service with the company, age, amount of schooling, the school the employee attended, and demonstration of the right attitude. For example, the young man who wants to go up the executive escalator smoothly tends to do so by quietly building up seniority and practicing *jicho*, "respecting himself." This means, again, that he will take every precaution not to invite criticism or attract undue attention to himself; he will never be forward nor question his superiors; and he will more or less merge himself with the furniture and wait his turn.

No doubt the key reason why the superior-subordinate ranking system in Japanese society is so powerful is because it makes everyone totally dependent on those above and below them. Each member must do his or her own part to avoid jeopardizing the entire group. With this in mind, it is not difficult to understand why a thirty-year-old assistant section chief in Mitsui & Company or Hitachi or Suzuki Electric is not about to disturb the harmony he has with his co-workers, inferiors, or superiors, since he is likely to spend his whole working life with them and his contentment and success depend upon their continuing goodwill.

Shikomu
Training in "Company Morality"

The Japanese like to say "The enterprise is the people," meaning that a company cannot be separated from the people who make it up; that is, members of a company are bound together by emotional, economic, and social ties that transcend all others. The Japanese do not believe an employee can or will make his full contribution to the enterprise unless he is totally committed to the company and gives it his highest loyalty. This is another reason why major Japanese firms prefer to hire employees directly from school, when they are young and "unspoiled" and more susceptible to being imbued with the company philosophy.

The training Japanese companies put new employees

through to instill their particular philosophy is referred to as *shikomu* (she-koe-muu), which is a special kind of training that includes not only techniques but also the morality and philosophy of the actions required to accomplish a job. The master carpenter in Old Japan, for example, would send his apprentice to the theater to learn the ethics of life. When the apprentice later made a mistake with the saw or hammer, the master would upbraid him and ask if he had not yet learned anything at the theater.

The Japanese philosophy is that the company with good human relations will succeed, while the company with bad human relations will fail. The smooth functioning of human relations within companies, at least in principle, takes precedence over what the section, department, or sometimes even the whole company is supposed to accomplish.

This human-relations type of management preferred by the Japanese is based on face-to-face physical contact within groups, and with individuals in other groups with whom they have established relations. This, of course, is another aspect of the role of introductions and go-betweens, and it explains why the Japanese business system precludes, or make difficult, conducting business by telephone until face-to-face contact has been made and a basis for a substantial degree of *amae* has been established.

Shakai No Kurabu
The Company as a Social Club

Akio Morita, one of the founders of the fabulously successful Sony Corporation, once remarked that Japanese companies "look" more like social organizations than business enterprises. Morita was, of course, referring not only to the junior-senior, parent-child vertical structure of Japanese companies but also to the famous "paternalism" of the larger ones.

To understand and work with a Japanese company, it is indeed helpful to think of it in terms of a combination of an exclusive club, a cooperative union, and last, a business enterprise because it incorporates attributes of all three.

Japanese industry as a whole is characterized by the existence of a few huge companies that dominate each particular industrial category and are usually aligned with a *zaibatsu*-like group of other firms. Beneath these giant companies is a thicker layer of medium-sized firms, some of them independent and others satellite to one of the larger enterprises. Way below these two upper layers is a mass of small to miniscule shop-factories that are mostly dependent on the larger firms for their day-to-day existence.

Ichi-ryu, Ni-ryu, San-ryu
First-class, Second-class, Third-class

All of Japan's enterprises across the board are first classified according to industrial category, then by size and market share, and finally by whatever group of companies the individual firm may be affiliated with. All the larger and more important firms in each industrial category are ranked by their fellow members, as well as others, in relation to their standing when compared with all other enterprises in the same category. A major company is called an *ichi-ryu* (ee-chee-re-yuu) or "first-class" company. A *ni-ryu* (nee-re-yuu) company is a "second-class" company; and a *san-ryu* (sahn-re-yuu) is a "third-class" company. Those below third class are seldom ranked.

The gap between first-class companies and most second-class firms is usually considerable, emphasizing that each industrial category in the country tends to be made up of a few very large firms and a large number of medium-size and small firms. The ranking of the firms in the second and third classes is not always as clear-cut as among the *ichi-ryu*, but the leading *ni-ryu* and *san-ryu* firms are very conscious of their relative ranking, and they continuously strive to elevate themselves to a higher class.

Competition for the title and prestige of *ichi-ryu* company is also intense—and continuous—often going beyond what Western businessmen regard as rational behavior. This is part of the motivation that spurs the Japanese economy.

Just as Japanese companies vie to achieve or maintain the highest rank, competition among young Japanese high school and college graduates to enter *ichi-ryu* companies is equally intense. Until recent years at least, working for a first-class company was more important to most Japanese than pure economic considerations, because social status was primarily determined by place of employment. Traditionally in Japan, social status took precedence over economic status, and still today the social motive often outranks the profit motive (a value many non-Japanese find hard to swallow). The prestige of working for a first-ranked company in Japan extends from the chief executive officers down to the lowest laborers, and in fact constitutes a kind of economic caste system.

Another characteristic of Japanese industry is for each of the larger firms to have a host of smaller subsidiary and affiliated subcontract (*shita-uke* [ssh-tah-uu-kay]) firms clustered around them. The subsidiary companies are known as *ko-gaisha* (koe-guy-shah) or "child-companies." There are two types of affiliated companies: *chokkei kigyo* (choke-kay-e keeg-yoe), or "direct-line" companies, and *keiretsu kaisha* (kay-e-rate-sue kie-shah) or "aligned companies." Direct-line companies in this terminology and practice resemble wholly owned subsidaries.

The relationship between "aligned" companies and the larger "parent" companies is less precise and less intimate. The parent company may supply capital to the aligned company and provide various marketing functions. The degree of the alignment, ultimately, is determined by the percentage of its production that it is obligated to sell to the parent company, which in turn determines its dependence on the larger firm.

Juyaku
"Big" Executives

As in most enterprises everywhere, there are three categories of personnel in a large Japanese company: the *jimukei* (jee-muu-kay-ee), or administrative personnel; the *gijutsu-kei* (ghee-jute-sue-kay-ee), or technical personnel; and the *ippan* (eep-pahn) or "common" staff. This is one of the few similarities between Japanese and non-Japanese firms. For one thing, larger Japanese companies hire only university graduates for administrative positions. Examples of junior and senior high school graduates making their way up the managerial hierarchy in Japan are rare indeed.

There are also three levels of employees in larger Japanese companies. These are the *yaku-in* (yah-kuu-eene), or executives from director on up; the *bukacho* (buu-kah-choe), or middle and lower management made up of department and section heads and their assistants; and the *hira-shain* (he-rah-shah-eene), or "level" employees, that is, those without rank. The following table gives the administrative titles (grades) commonly found in larger Japanese companies:

Kabunushi (Kah-buu-nuu-she)	Stockholders
Torishimariyakukai (Toe-ree-she-mah-ree-yah-kuu-kie)	Board of Directors
Kaicho (Kie-choe)	Chairman of the Board
Daihyo Torishimariyaku (Die-h'yoe Toe-ree-she-mah-ree-yah-kuu)	Representative Director
Shacho (Shah-choe)	President
Senmu Torishimariyaku (Sane-muu Toe-ree-she-mah-ree-yah-kuu)	Director & Executive Vice-President
Jomu Torishimariyaku (Joe-muu Toe-ree-she-mah-ree-yah-kuu)	Director & Senior Vice-President
Jonin Kansayaku (Joe-neen Khan-sah-yah-kuu)	Standing Auditor
Bucho (Buu-choe)	Department Head
Kacho (Kah-choe)	Section Head
Kakaricho (Kah-kah-ree-choe)	Supervisor
Hira-shain (Hc-rah-shah-eene)	Unranked Employees

Each Japanese company usually has one or more *daihyo torishimariyaku*—directors who have power of attorney to act in the name of the company. Besides the regular *bucho* (department chiefs), companies may also have *senmon bucho* (sane-moan buu-choe), or "specialty department heads"—individuals who have been promoted to *bucho* because of their professional skill or knowledge but have no department under them. In large companies, some *bucho* may also be corporate directors.

Hako-No Naka Ni Hitobito
People in Boxes

The basic organizational and operating unit in most large Japanese companies is a section or subsection made up of several persons. Each section *(ka)* consists of a section chief *(kacho)*, usually two assistants or supervisors *(kakaricho)*, and several staff members. Several sections combined make up a department *(bu)*, headed by a department chief *(bucho)*.

The physical makeup in a section is a "box"—desks arranged to form a rectangular box-shape, with the manager and his assistants at the front or head of the formation and the junior members strung out along the sides. Each department is made up of several of these "boxes."

The desk of the department chief is usually the farthest from the door, near a window if there is one, commanding a good view of the entire department. Generally, the only managers in a large Japanese company who have private offices are executive directors and up.

Within each of these basic boxes, responsibility and activity is more or less a team effort, with work assigned to the group as a whole. Members of each section are expected to cooperate and support one another. Older, more experienced members provide new members with the direction and help they need in a continuous on-the-job training process. The effectiveness of a particular section is strongly influenced by the morale, ambition, and talent of the whole team.

Just as individuals within the section "boxes" are ranked according to their seniority and title (and unofficially according to their overall attitude and effectiveness), the "boxes" are also ranked according to their importance within the departments they make up. The larger the number of people in a box, the more important that section is likely to be. The more sections in a department, the more important that department.

Managers are very much aware of the rank of their sections

and departments, and they are naturally concerned about being assigned to a section or department ranked below what they "know" their own seniority and experience deserve.

This organizational structure within a Japanese company is rigid and, therefore, does not contribute to speedy results or innovations. To counter this handicap, Japanese companies also make use of special project teams to cope with and take advantage of new technological and management developments, leading some critics of the present system to predict that these teams will eventually replace the "box-sections" altogether.

Bu
Finding the Right One

Most of the departments in Japanese companies are similar in name to comparable departments in Western companies. In function, however, there are some outstanding exceptions. Namely, the general affairs department, or *somu bu* (soh-muu buu), and the personnel department or *jinji bu* (jeen-jee buu).

The *somu bu* has no exact counterpart in Western firms, but it is a key department in most large Japanese enterprises. It does such things as provide liaison with customers, coordinate interdepartmental relations, handle company mail, and oversee the telephone switchboards, maintenance, official files, stock ledgers, etc. It is the *somu bu* that provides receptionists who greet callers; so most initial contacts with major Japanese companies are with this department.

The *jinji bu* or personnel department in a Japanese company is generally larger and much more powerful than its counterpart in a Western company. It makes practically all decisions as to who is hired, where they are initially assigned, and when and where they are rotated as part of their continuous on-the-job training.

Other typical departments in larger Japanese companies are as follows:

Kokusai Bu (Koke-sie Buu)   International Department
Seizo Bu (Say-e-zoe Buu)   Production Department
Kikaku Bu (Kee-kah-kuu Buu)   Planning Department

Shizai Bu (Shee-zie Buu)	Purchasing Department
Shogai Bu (Show-guy Buu)	Public Relations Department
Keiri Bu (Kay-e-ree Buu)	Accounting Department
Eigyo Bu (Aa-e-g'yoe Buu)	Sales Department
Koho Bu (Koe-hoe Buu)	Advertising Department

Even though the names of these departments are familiar, they, like the management categories, have their own unique Japanese character.

In addition to the various *bu* (departments), some large Japanese firms also have what is called the *Shacho Shitsu* (Shah-choe Sheet-sue) or "President's Room." This is a team that performs staff work for the president of the company. The functions of the *Shacho Shitsu* vary in different firms, and they may include secretarial work, record-keeping, planning, and management information systems.

The grouping or sectionalization by and within Japanese organizations has a number of serious drawbacks in the conduct of business. It hinders and, in many instances, completely blocks communication, not only within the individual groups themselves but also between groups, including those in the same organization or enterprise. The reason for this is that in an exclusive, tightly knit, vertically aligned group, communication is more or less limited to moving upward or downward, and in most cases it must go through every senior member in each level of the hierarchy. If one member is absent or chooses not to act, the communication may be short-circuited. This vertical structure also makes horizontal communication with "outsiders" difficult because individual links in the structure are generally not authorized to make decisions or engage in business negotiations on their own.

Even the top man cannot act as a spokesman for the group without first reaching a consensus of opinion among his co-workers and fellow managers, regardless of the subject matter. This process of consensus naturally takes time and also incorporates the possibility that there may be no response, since it is more difficult to get five or seven or more people to agree on anything. This is also one of the primary reasons why it is usually difficult for an outsider (a journalist, for example) to call up a Japanese company and receive any kind of official policy statement or sometimes just a simple detail about the company's activities.

Another disadvantge of the *sempai-kohai,* or senior-junior, grouping system is that its exclusivity contributes to the non-cooperative spirit and even hostility with which the Japanese view outsiders. Since they are bound to the group, members do not want anyone upsetting its balance or harmony in any way. There is thus very little and sometimes no communication between departments on a staff level. This sectionalism is so intense in some organizations that a kind of internal warfare rages. Rivalry between sections and departments in service-type companies, such as public relations and advertising, is often especially fierce, making it even more difficult for the client or customer who must deal with more than one group in the company.

Further, a management system based on personal loyalty within a group and on seniority makes it very difficult for Japanese managers to shift from job to job, or from company to company, even when they have the still rare opportunity to do so. The emotions aroused when this system is ignored or breaks down—as happened in many joint Japanese-foreign venture operations established in the past three decades—invariably leads to unsatisfactory if not disastrous results. Being very much aware of these dangers, really topflight Japanese managers generally try to avoid being assigned to joint ventures, leaving them to "second-string" managers or to those who are near or already in forced retirement.

The problems involved in forming a new company with "old" employees in Japan are formidable. The Japanese often accept the premise that the managers first assigned to such undertakings are little more than caretakers. They take a long-range view, resigning themselves to wait several years for capable people to come up from the bottom in the new enterprise.

Despite its failings, however, the grouping system in Japanese business management results in motivation that is both powerful and dynamic. Like the villagers of feudal Japan who could raise their social status only by outproducing their neighbors, members of the individual groups in Japanese companies can enhance their own prestige only by increasing the effectiveness and importance of their group. This instills in each member a powerful urge not only to protect the rights and interests of the group, but also to make it stand out from competing sections.

Bo Nen Kai
Meeting to Forget

Japan's personally oriented management system, with its strict rules requiring workers to repress their individualism in the interest of group harmony, naturally results in friction and the buildup of stress. There are two popular annual activities partly aimed at helping to relieve the personal antagonisms that develop among group and company members: the *Bo Nen Kai* (Boe Nane Kie), "Forget the Old Year Party," and the *Shin Nen Kai* (Sheen Nane Kie), "New Year Party."

The theme of the traditional end-of-the-year *Bo Nen Kai* party, held at the place of work and marked by food and drinks, is to have a good time with co-workers and forgive and forget all the bad things that happened during the course of the year. There is no set date for the "Forget the Old Year Party." Some companies hold them several days before the last working day of the year.

New Year's, *Osho Gatsu* (Oh-show Got-sue), is Japan's most important holiday. Almost everyone is off work for three or four days, and some companies close for longer periods. The occasion is used for family and shrine visits. In most offices and companies on the first day after the New Year's break, there is an informal open-house-type *Shin Nen Kai*, or "New Year Meeting." The purpose of the meeting is for workers and managers to formally greet one another and ask for goodwill, cooperation, and help for another year. The idea is to start each new year on a positive note so as to contribute to both morale and productivity the rest of the year. Usually little or no work is done on this day. Women employees, particularly younger ones, often wear their prettiest kimono on this occasion.

It is also customary at this time of year for company representatives to visit their banks* and for suppliers to visit companies that buy from them. The callers first greet their contacts with, *Akemashite Shin Nen O'medeto Gozaimasu* (Ah-kay-mah-ssh-tay Sheen Nane Oh-may-day-toe Go-zie-mahss)— "Congratulations on the Opening of the New Year" or "Happy New Year!"

This is immediately followed by the set expression: *Saku nen chu wa taihen Osewa ni narimashita. Mata kon nen mo yoroshiku Onegai itashimasu* (Sah-kuu nane chuu wah tie-hane Oh-say-wah nee nah-ree-mahssh-tah. Mah-tah kone nane moe yoe-row-she-kuu Oh-nay-guy ee-tah-she-mahss). This means, loosely, "We are deeply obligated to you for your patronage and help last year, and extend our deepest gratitude. We ask that you please continue doing business with us this year."

---

*Japanese businessmen are generally much more deeply obligated to their banks than are their foreign counterparts. Many banks also own substantial equity in anywhere from a few to dozens of companies.

5

Manejimento
Aspects of Japanese Company Management

Shu-Shin Koyo
It's for Life

Probably the most talked about and notorious facet of Japan's family-patterned company system is *shu-shin koyo* (shuu-sheen koe-yoe), or "lifetime employment," which applies, however, to only an elite minority of the nation's workers. Although a direct descendant of feudal Japan, when peasants and craftsmen were attached to a particular clan by birth, the lifetime employment system did not become characteristic of large-scale modern Japanese industry until the 1950s. In the immediate postwar period, losing one's job was tantamount to being sentenced to starvation. To prevent employees from being fired or arbitrarily laid off, national federation union leaders took advantage of their new freedom and the still weak position of industry to force adoption of the lifetime employment system by the country's major enterprises.

Under the lifetime employment system, all *permanent* employees of larger companies and government bureaus are, in practice, hired for life. These organizations generally hire only once a year, directly from schools. Well before the end of the school year, each company and government ministry or

71

agency decides on how many new people it wants to bring in. The company or government bureau then invites students who are to graduate that year (in some cases only from certain universities) to take written and oral examinations for employment.

One company, for example, may plan on taking 200 university graduates as administrative trainees, and 500 junior and senior high school graduates for placement in blue-collar work. Since "permanent" employment is "for life," companies are careful to select candidates who have well-rounded personalities and are judged most likely to adjust to that particular company or agency's philosophy and "style."

This method of employee selection is known as *Shikaku Seido* or "Personal Qualifications System." This means that new employees are selected on the basis of their education, character, personality, and family backgrounds; as opposed to work experience or technological backgrounds.

A larger Japanese company hiring new employees, as well as firms entering into new business tie-ups, are sometimes compared to *miai kekkon* or "arranged marriages." The analogy is a good one. Both employment and joint-venture affiliations are, in principle, for life. Therefore, both parties want to be sure not only of the short-term intentions of the potential partner but also of the character and personality—even if there are any "black sheep" in the family. Thus both prospective employee and potential business partner must undergo close scrutiny. When the Japanese commit themselves, the commitment is expected to be total.

Choosing employees on the basis of personal qualifications is especially important to Japanese supervisors and managers, because they personally cannot hire, fire, or hold back promotions. They must acquire and keep the trust, goodwill, and cooperation of their subordinates, and manage by example and tact.

Besides exercising control over employee candidates by allowing only students from certain universities to take their entrance examinations, many companies in Japan also depend upon well-known professors in specific universities to recommend choice candidates to them each year. The reputations of some professors, especially in the physical sciences, are often such that they can actually "parcel out" the best students from their graduating classes to top firms in their field.

Nenko Joretsu
The "Merit of Years"

Once hired by a larger company, the permanent Japanese employee who is a university graduate is on the first rung of a pay/promotion escalator system that over the years will gradually and automatically take him to or near the upper management level. This is the famous (or infamous) *nenko joretsu* (nane-koe joe-ray-t'sue), "long-service rank" or seniority system, under which pay and promotions are primarily based on longevity.

Not surprisingly, the employee, at least in administrative areas, is considered more important than the job in the Japanese company system. As a result, job classifications on the administrative level may be clear enough, but specific duties of individuals tend to be ill-defined or not defined at all. Work is more or less assigned on a collective basis, and each employee tends to work according to his or her ability and inclinations. Those who are capable, diligent, and ambitious naturally do most of the work. Those who turn out to be lazy or incompetent are given tasks befitting their abilities and interests.

Young management trainees are switched from one job to another every two or three years, and in larger companies they are often transferred to other offices or plants. The reason for this is to expose them to a wide range of experiences so they will be more valuable to the company as they go up the promotion ladder. Individuals are "monitored" and informally rated, and eventually the more capable are promoted faster than the other members of their age group. The ones promoted the fastest usually become managing directors; and one of their number generally becomes president.

During the first twelve to fifteen years of employment, the most capable junior managers accrue status instead of more pay raises and faster promotions. If they prove to be equally capable in their personal relations with others, they are the ones who are eventually singled out to reach the upper levels of the managerial hierarchy.

The seniority system in Japanese companies takes ordinary, even incapable, people who have toed the company line and made no blunders, to the head of departments, and occasionally to the head of companies. But their limitations are recognized, and the department or company is run by competent people below them, with little or no damage to the egos of the less capable executives or to the overall harmony within the firm.

Each work-section of a Japanese company is three-layered, consisting of young, on-the-job trainees (a status that often lasts for several years); mature, experienced workers who carry most of the burden; and older employees whose productivity has fallen off due to their age.

Direct, specific orders do not set well with the members of these work-sections. Such orders leave them with the impression they are not trusted and that mangement has no respect for them. Even the lowest clerk or delivery boy in a company is very sensitive about being treated with respect. The Japanese say they prefer general "ambiguous" instructions. All that work-groups want from management "are goals and direction."

Because human relations are given precedence in the Japanese management system, great importance is attached to the "unity of employees" within each of these groups. The primary responsibility of the senior manager in a group is not to direct the people in their work but to make "adjustments" among them in order to maintain harmonious relations within the group.

"What is required of the ideal manager," say the Japanese, "is that he know how to adjust human relations rather than be knowledgeable about the operation of his department or the overall function of the company. In fact, the man who is competent and works hard is not likely to be popular with other members of his group and as a result does not make a good manager," they add.

Besides "appearing somewhat incompetent" as far as work is concerned while being skilled at preventing interemployee friction, the ideal Japanese manager has one other important trait. He is willing to shoulder all the responsibility for any mistakes or failings of his subordinates—hoping, of course, there will be no loss of face.

The efficient operation of this group system is naturally based on personal obligations and trust between the manager and his staff. The manager must make his staff obligated to him in order to keep their cooperation and in order to ensure that none of them will deliberately do anything or leave anything undone that would cause him embarrassment. Whatever knowledge and experience are required for the group to be productive is found among the manager's subordinates if he is weak in this area.

Seishin
Training in Spirit

The Japanese associate productivity with employees having *seishin* (say-e-sheen), or "spirit," and being imbued with "Japanese morality." Company training, therefore, covers not only technical areas but also moral, philosophical, aesthetic, and political factors. Each of the larger companies has its own particular company philosophy and image, which are incorporated into its training and indoctrination programs. This is one of the prime reasons why major Japanese companies prefer not to hire older, experienced "outsiders"; it is assumed that they could not wholly accept or fit into the company mold.

Onjo Shugi
"Mothering" Employees

The amount of loyalty, devotion, and hard work displayed by most Japanese employees is in direct proportion to the paternalism, *onjo shugi* (own-joe shuu-ghee), of the company management system. The more paternalistic (maternalistic would seem to be a better word) the company, the harder working and the more devoted and loyal employees tend to be. Japanese-style paternalism includes the concept that the employer is totally responsible for the livelihood and well-being of all employees and must be willing to go all the way for an employee when the need arises.

The degree of paternalism in Japanese companies varies tremendously, with some of them literally practicing cradle-to-grave responsibility for employees and their families. Many managers thus spend a great deal of time participating in social events involving their staff members—births, weddings, funerals, and so on.

Fringe benefits make up a very important part of the income of most Japanese workers, and they include such things as housing or housing subsidies, transportation allowances, family allowances, child allowances, health services, free recreational facilities, educational opportunities, retirement funds, etc.

The wide range of fringe benefits received by Japanese employees is an outgrowth of spiraling inflation and an increasingly heavy income tax system during the years between 1945 and 1955. Companies first began serving employees free lunches. Then larger companies built dormitories, apartments, and houses. Eventually, recreational, educational, and medical facilities were added to employee benefits.

Japan's famous twice-a-year bonuses, *shoyo* (show-yoe), were originally regarded as a fringe benefit by employees and management, but workers and unions have long since considered them an integral part of wages. Unions prefer to call the bonuses *kimatsu teate* (kee-mot-sue tay-ah-tay), or "seasonal allowances." The bonuses, usually the equivalent of two to six or eight months of base wages, are paid in midsummer just before *Obon* (Oh-bone), a major Buddhist festival honoring the dead, and just before the end of the calendar year in December.

Rinji Saiyo
The Outsiders

Not all employees of Japanese companies, including the larger ones, are hired for life or come under the *nenko joretsu* system of pay and promotion. There are two distinct categories of employees in most Japanese companies: those who are hired as permanent employees under the *shu-shin koyo* and *nenko joretsu* systems, and those hired under the *rinji saiyo* or "temporary appointment" system. The latter may be hired by the day or by the year, but they cannot be hired on contract for more than one year at a time. They are paid at a lower scale than permanent employees and may be laid off or fired at any time.

The *rinji saiyo* system of temporary employees is, of course, a direct outgrowth of the disadvantages of a permanent employment system, which at most is viable only in a booming, continuously growing economy.

The rapid internationalization of Japan's leading corporations is also having a profound effect on their policies regarding young Japanese who have graduated from foreign universities. Until the mid-1980s most Japanese companies simply would not consider hiring someone who had been partly or wholly educated abroad. Their rationale was that such people were no longer one hundred percent Japanese and, therefore, would not fit into the training programs or the environment of Japanese companies.

Now a growing number of Japanese corporations with large international operations are looking for young people who have been educated abroad, speak a foreign language, and already have experience in living overseas. Ricoh, for example, now has a regular policy of hiring some of its annual crop of new employees from the group of Japanese students attending American universities.

Several Japanese employment agencies are now active among Japanese students in the U.S., providing them with information about job opportunities with Japanese companies overseas.

Jimusho No Hana
"Office Flowers"

Women, mostly young, make up a highly visible percentage of Japan's labor force, particularly in offices (where they are often referred to as *jimsho no hana* or "office flowers") and in light manufacturing industries requiring precision handwork. Most of these young women are expected to leave the work force when they get married, but increasing numbers of them are staying on after marriage, at least until they begin having children, and are returning to the labor force after their children are raised.

Equally significant is that, little by little, women are beginning to cross the barrier between staff and management, and participate in the heady world of planning and decision-making.

While female managers are still generally confined to such industries as public relations, advertising, publishing, and retailing, economic and social pressures are gradually forcing other industries as well to begin thinking about desegregating their male-only management systems.

Another highly conspicuous phenomenon in Japan today is the growing number of women who head up their own successful companies in such areas as real estate, cosmetics, apparel, and the food business.

The world of Japanese business is still very much a male preserve, however, with many of the relationships and rituals that make up a vital part of daily business activity still closed to women. There are virtually no women in the numerous power groups, factions, clubs, and associations that characterize big business in Japan.

Foreign women who choose to do business in or with Japan face most of the same barriers that handicap Japanese women. They are unable to participate in the ritualistic after-work drinking and partying that are a major part of developing and maintaining effective business relations within the Japanese system. They cannot transcend their sex and be accepted as business persons first and foremost. They are unable to deal with other women on a managerial level in other companies simply because there generally are none.

They must also face the fact that most Japanese executives have had no experience in dealing with female managers, have no protocol for doing so, and are inclined to believe that women are not meant to be business managers in the first place.

This does not mean that foreign women cannot successfully engage in business in Japan, but they must understand the barriers, be able to accept them for what they are, and work around them. If they come on strong, as women or as managers, to Japanese businessmen who are traditionally oriented, they will most likely fail. They must walk a much finer line than men.

At the same time, a foreign woman who is both attractive and really clever in knowing how to use her femininity to manipulate men can succeed in Japan where others fail. This approach can be especially effective if the woman concerned is taken under the wing of an older, powerful Japanese businessman who likes her and takes a personal interest in her success.

Perhaps the most important lesson the foreign businesswoman in Japan must learn is that the Japanese regard business as a personal matter, and believe that the personal element must be satisfied before any actual business transpires. This means she must go through the process of establishing emotional rapport with her male Japanese counterparts, and convince them that she is a knowledgeable, experienced, trustworthy, and dependable business person.

It is often difficult for foreign men to develop this kind of relationship with Japanese businessmen, particularly when language is a problem, so the challenge to foreign women who want to do business in Japan (unless they go just as buyers or artists, etc.) is formidable.

The type of foreign woman who is most likely to do well in the Japanese environment is one who has a genuine affinity for the language and the culture, and appreciates both the opportunities and challenges offered by the situation. She must also have an outstanding sense of humor, be patient and be willing to suppress some of her rational, liberal feelings.

Ringi Seido
Putting It in Writing

In addition to the cooperative-work approach based on each employee contributing according to his or her ability and desire, many large Japanese companies divide and diversify management responsibility by a system known as *ringi seido* (reen-ghee say-ee-doe), which means, more or less, "written proposal system." This is a process by which management decisions are based on proposals made by lower level managers, and it is responsible for the "bottoms-up" management associated with many Japanese companies.

Briefly, the *ringi* system consists of proposals written by the initiating section or department that are circulated horizontally and vertically to all layers of management for approval. Managers and executives who approve of the proposal stamp the document with their *hanko* (hahn-koe) name seals in the prescribed place. Anyone who disapproves either passes the document on without stamping it or puts his seal on it sideways or upside down to indicate conditional approval.

When approval is not unanimous, higher executives may send the document back with recommendations that more staff work be done on it or that the opinions of those who disapprove be taken into consideration. Manager may attach comments to the proposal if they wish.

In practice, the man who originates a *ringi-sho* (written proposal document) informally consults with other managers before submitting it for official scrutiny. He may work for weeks or months in his efforts to get the idea approved unofficially. If he runs into resistance, he will invariably seek help from colleagues who owe him favors. They in turn will approach others who are obligated to them.

The efficiency and effectiveness of the *ringi seido* varies with the company. In some it is little more than a formality, and there is pressure from the top to eliminate the system altogether. In other companies the system reigns supreme, and there is strong opposition to any talk of eliminating it. The system is so deeply entrenched in both the traditional management philosophy of the Japanese and the aspirations and ambitions of younger managers that it will no doubt be around for a long time.

The foreign businessman negotiating with a Japanese company should be aware that his proposals may be the subject of one or more *ringi-sho* which not only takes up a great deal of time (they must be circulated in the proper chain-of-status order), it alo exposes them to the scrutiny of as many as a dozen or more individuals whose interests and attitudes may differ.

Whether or not a *ringi* proposal is approved by the president is primarily determined by who has aproved it by the time it gets to him. If all or most of the more important managers concerned have stamped the *ringi-sho,* chances are the president will also approve it.

While this system is cumbersome and slow, generally speaking it helps build and maintain a cooperative spirit within companies. In addition, it assures that when a policy change or new progam is initiated, it will have the support of the majority of managers.

As can be seen from the still widespread use of the *ringi seido,* top managers in many Japanese companies are not always planners and decision-makers. Their main function is to see that the company operates smoothly and efficiently as a team, to see that new managers are nurtured within the system, and to "pass judgment" on proposals made by junior managers.

Nemawashi
Behind the Scenes

Just as the originator of a *ringi* proposal will generally not submit it until he is fairly sure it will be received favorably, Japanese managers in general do not, unlike their foreign counterparts, hold formal meetings to discuss subjects and make decisions. They meet to agree formally on what has already been decided in informal discussions behind the scenes.

These informal discussions are called *nemawashi* (nay-mah-wah-she) or "binding up the roots"—to make sure a plant's roots are protected when it is transplanted.

Nemawashi protocol does not require that all managers who might be concerned be consulted. But agreement must always be obtained from the "right" person—meaning the individual in the department, division, or upper echelon of the company management—who really exercises power.

Kaigi
Talk Meets

Since business management in Japan is more of a consensus process, Japanese managers probably have twice as many meetings, *kaigi* (kie-ghee), as their counterparts in the West. Some standard ones are the following:

Tori Shimariyaku Kai	Board of Directors' Meeting
(Toe-ree She-mah-ree-yah-kuu Kie)	
Juyaku Kai Juu-yah-kuu Kie)	Directors' Meeting
Bucho Kai (Buu-choe Kie)	Dept. Heads' Meeting
I-in Kai (Ee-een Kie)	Committee Meeting

Juyaku Ga Nai
"No Executives in Japan"

One authority on Japanese management makes the rather astounding observation that while there are "business managers" in Japan, there are no "business executives" in the Western sense. Masaaki Imai, managing director of Cambridge Research Institute-Japan, says that in a situation where employment is permanent and management is collective, there can be "no such thing" as an executive. Imai explains:

> In a way, every white collar employee in a company is an executive, and everyone is not. When a university graduate joins a company, he knows that some 13 to 15 years later he will be promoted to *kacho* (section chief), even if his first assignment is clipping newspapers. So do all of his colleagues who joined the company when he did.
>
> Thus from the standpoint of the individual, the transition from employee to "executive" is automatic. Until he is promoted to *kacho* level, he belongs to the union and makes such demands as pay raises to the management. One morning he wakes up to find he has become a *kacho*, and starts dealing with the union on behalf of the company . . .
>
> . . . Whether a Japanese is an executive or not is not so much derived from his own will and effort, but from the years he has spent in the company.

Imai adds that many companies often reserve important

management positions for union leaders for the day when they stop being union leaders. (In Japan, most unions are "company unions" as opposed to craft or trade unions.)

The role of the *juyaku* (juu-yah-kuu) or "Big Executive" in typical, large Japanese companies is also quite different from that in comparable American companies. Most major Japanese firms select the members of their Board of Directors, *Tori Shimari Yakkai* (Toe-ree She-mah-ree Yaak-kie), from within their own company. The boards are generally made up of the president of the particular company and other line executives down to and including some *bu cho* (department chiefs). The function of the board is mostly ceremonial, and the title of "director" is primarily "social."

The board that really runs the large Japanese company—if one does—is the *Jomu Kai* (Joe-muu Kie) or "Managing Directors' Board." This board is made up of the heads of key departments, with the president as the chairman. Most *Jomu Kai* are little more than rubber-stamp boards, however, that are dominated by one man because the *sempai-kohai*, or senior-junior, system invariably prevails.

Hanko
Chopping People Down

The Japanese have traditionally used *hanko* (hahn-koe), name stamps, seals, or "chops," in lieu of written signatures when signing contracts and other types of formal or official documents. Especially where government bureaus and agencies are concerned, up to a dozen or more individuals in as many departments may be required to stamp a document, sometimes several times each in different places.

The mechanics of the practice by itself are irksome, often to an extreme degree, but it is usually something that time and great patience can surmount—if no hitches develop. Among the problems that can and do develop regularly: one (or more) of the people whose stamp is required is not available and following their hierarchical habit of grading everything, the name seals may have to go on in a prescribed order, causing long delays; someone decides he is not going to cooperate because he disapproves of the document, the person who originated it, or because he may be feuding with some of the other managers, etc.

Foreign businessmen living and working in Japan have the right to get a *hanko* stamp made and, if it is registered *(natsuin)* (not-sue-een), use it as their official signature. But few go to the trouble since the foreigner is allowed to write out his name—although in some cases the signing has to be certified before it is legal. Also, the *hanko* present a security problem since they can bind their owners to a contract even if affixed without their knowledge or authorization.

While written signatures are now the rule in international business in Japan, the *hanko* is still something to be reckoned with in dealings within the confines of Japanese companies and with government agencies, and it is likely to remain so for some time.

Mibun
The Rights Have It

Everybody in Japan has his or her *mibun* (me-boon), "personal rights" or "station in life," and every *bun* has its special rights and responsibilities. There are special rights and special restrictions applying to managers only, to students only, to teachers only, to workers only, etc. The restrictions of a particular category are usually clear-cut and are intended to control the behavior of the people within these categories at all times—for example, the office employee even when he is not working or the student when he isn't in school.

The traditional purpose of the feudalistic *mibun* concept was to maintain harmony within and between different categories of people. A second purpose was to prevent anyone from bringing discredit or shame upon his category or his superiors.

A good example of the *mibun* system at work was once told by Konosuke Matsushita, founder of the huge Matsushita Electric Company (Panasonic, National, etc). At the age of ten, Matsushita was apprenticed to a bicycle shop, which meant that he was practically a slave, forced to work from five in the morning until bedtime.

In addition to his regular duties, Matsushita had to run to a tobacco store several times a day for customers who came into the bicycle shop. Before he could go, however, he had to wash. After several months of this, he hit upon the idea of buying several packs of cigarettes at one time, with his own meager savings, so that when a customer asked for tobacco, he not only could hand it to him immediately but also profit a few *sen* on each pack, since he received a discount by buying twenty packs at a time.

This pleased not only the bicycle shop customers but also Matsushita's master, who complimented him highly on his ingenuity. A few days later, however, the master of the shop told him that all the other workers were complaining about his enterprise and that he would have to stop it and return to the old system.

It was not within the *bun* of a mere flunky to demonstrate such ability.

The aims of foreign businessmen are often thwarted because they attempt to get things done by Japanese whose *bun* does not allow them to do whatever is necessary to accomplish the desired task. Instead of telling the businessmen they cannot do it or passing the matter on to someone who can, there is a tendency for the individual to wait a certain period, or until they are approached again by the businessmen, then announce that it is impossible.

In any dealings with a Japanese company, it is especially important to know the *bun* of the people representing the firm. The Japanese businessman who does have individual authority is often buttressed behind subordinates whose *bun* are strictly limited. If the outsider isn't careful, a great deal of time can be wasted on the wrong person.

It is the special freedoms or "rights" of the *bun* system that cause the most trouble. As is natural everywhere, the Japanese minimize the responsibilities of their *bun* and emphasize the rights, with the result that there are detailed and well-known rules outlining the rights of each catgegory, but few rules covering the responsibilities.

As one disillusioned bureaucrat-turned-critic put it, "The rights of government and company bureaucrats tend to be limitless, while responsibilities are ignored or passed on to underlings. The underlings in turn say they are powerless to act without orders from above—or that it isn't their responsibility." The same critic also said that the only ability necessary to become a bureaucrat was that of escaping reponsibility without being criticized.

A story related by a former editor of one of Japan's better known intellectual magazines illustrates how the *mibun* system penetrates into private life. While still an editor with the magazine, Mr. S went out one night for a few drinks with a very close writer-friend. While they were drinking, another writer, the noted Mr. D, came into the bar and joined them.

Mr. S continues: "I was not 'in charge' of Mr. D in my publishing house and didn't know him very well, but according to Japanese etiquette I should have bowed to him, paid him all kinds of high compliments and told him how much I was obligated to him. But it was long after my working hours and I was enjoying a drink with a friend who was also a writer, so I just bowed and paid little attention to him.

"At this, Mr. D became angry and commanded me in a loud voice to go home. I refused to move and he began shouting curses at me. I shouted back at him that I was drinking with a friend and it was none of his business, but he continued to abuse me loudly until my friend finally managed to quiet him down. Of course, I would have been fired the next day except that my friend was able to keep Mr. D from telling the directors of my company."

In doing business with a Japanese firm, it is important to find out the rank of each individual you deal with so you can determine the extent of his *bun*. It is also vital that you know the status of his particular section or department, which has its own ranking within the company.

There are other management characteristics that make it especially difficult for the uninitiated foreigner to deal with Japanese companies, including barriers to fast, efficient communication between levels of management within the companies. Everything must go through the proper chain of command, in a carefully prescribed, ritualistic way. If any link in this vertical chain is missing—away on business or sick—routine communication usually stops there. The ranking system does not allow Japanese management to delegate authority or responsibility to any important extent. Generally, one person cannot speak for another.

In fact, some Japanese observers have begun criticizing the consensus system of business and political management, saying its absolute power represents a major threat to Japan in that it prevents rapid decision-making and often makes it impossible for the Japanese to react swiftly enough to either problems or opportunities.

Hishokan
Where Are All the Secretaries?

As most Western businessmen would readily admit, they simply could not get along without their secretaries. In many ways, secretaries are as important, if not more so, than the executives themselves. In Japan only the rare businessman has a secretary whose role approximates the function of the Western secretary.

The reason for the scarcity of secretaries in Japan is manyfold. The style of Japanese management—the collective work-groups, decision-making by consensus, face-to-face communication, and the role of the manager as harmony-keeper instead of director—practically precludes the secretarial function. Another factor is the language itself, and the different language levels demanded by the subordinate-superior system. Japanese does not lend itself to clear, precise instructions because of the requirements of etiquette. It cannot be transcribed easily or quickly, either in shorthand or by typewriter—although the appearance of Japanese-language computers in the early 1980s is beginning to change that.

As a result, the Japanese are not prepared psychologically or practically for doing business through or with secretaries. The closest the typical Japanese company comes to having secretaries in the American sense are receptionists—usually pretty, young girls who are stationed at desks in building lobbies and in central floor and hall areas. They announce visitors who arrive with appointments and try to direct people who come in on business without specific apointments to the right section or department. When a caller who has never had any business with the company, and has no appointment, appears at one of the reception desks, the girl usually tries to line him up with someone in the General Affairs *(Somu Bu)* Department.

Small Japanese companies and many departments in larger companies do not have receptionists. In such cases, no specific individual is responsible for greeting and taking care of callers. The desks nearest the door are usually occupied by the lowest ranking members in the department, and it is usually up to the caller to get the attention of one of them and make his business known.

Shigoto
It's Not the Slot

The importance of face-to-face meetings in the conduct of business in Japan has already been mentioned. Regular, personal contact is also essential in maintaining "established relations" (the ability to *amaeru*) with business contacts. The longer two people have known each other and the more often they personally meet, the firmer this relationship.

This points up a particular handicap many foreign companies operating in Japan inadvertently impose on themselves by switching their personnel every two, three, or four years. In the normal course of business in Japan, it takes at least two years and sometimes as many as five years before the Japanese begin to feel like they really know their foreign employer, supplier, client, or colleague.

It also generally takes the foreign businessman transferred to Japan anywhere from one to three years or so to learn enough to really become effective in his job. Shortly afterward, he is transferred, recalled to the head office, is fired, or quits, and is replaced by someone else.

American businessmen in particular tend to pay too little attention to the disruption caused by personnel turnover, apparently because they think more in terms of the "position" or "slot" being filled by a "body" that has whatever qualifications the job calls for. Generally speaking, they play down the personality and character of the person filling the position and often do not adequately concern themselves with the role of human relations in business.

This, of course, is just the opposite of the Japanese way of doing things, and it accounts for a great deal of the friction that develops between Japanese and Westerners in business matters.

Tsushin
Don't Call Me . . .

One of the most common complaints about Japanese companies is that they often fail to answer business inquiries or requests for information. There are, of course, two sides to the story. Many Japanese companies receive hundreds of letters every week from all over the world. Some of the inquiries are from large, reputable firms. Others are from small companies trying to get started in business—ranging from retail shops to private individuals. The letters from abroad come in many different languages, including such lesser known ones as Urdu, Swahili, Tagalog, and Tamil.

Imagine, if you will, how many American, British, or French companies that receive dozens of letters from unknown sources, frequently in rare languages, would bother to do anything with them. But over and above this consideration, there are several reasons why written inquiries to Japanese companies are often not answered.

The individual Japanese section or department manager does not have a secretary or even a "pool" typist to take care of correspondence. Inquiries coming from abroad, unless they are addressed to a specific individual in a section or department, most likely go to the General Affairs Department, where they tend to end up in the hands of young employees who are still undergoing on-the-job training. They generally do not read English very well, much less other foreign languages, and may or may not spend hours with a foreign-language dictionary trying to decipher what the letters say. Most letters to Japanese companies do not go beyond this point.

Besides this, it is not customary for Japanese companies to provide information about their products or services to unknown outsiders (except for the annual reports, catalogs, or flyers available on special occasions). The reaction tends to be, "Who wants to know, and why?"

Another factor that works against Japanese companies "automatically" answering inquiries from unknown parties is that individual managers, and certainly not clerks, generally do not have the authority to provide information or make offers on their own. The Japanese manager can either say no or do nothing—which is the same thing, especially if he doesn't refer the request or proposition to someone else—but he cannot expose the company or commit the company to anything by himself.

The tendency of Japanese companies to be closed-mouthed and even secretive about their business is a result of several cultural and economic factors. Traditionally, Japanese society has been closed—made up of exclusive groups and groups within groups, each one very sensitive about its existence, responsibilities, and privileges, and basically hostile to all other groups, and to some degree in competition with them.

This system, and the ethics responsible for its development, precludes the free and open exchange of information between groups, since the primary motivation is to protect one's own group and outdo all others. This attitude and practice still prevails to a formidable degree in Japan's business world today.

Of course there are exceptions, since there are over 4,000 trading companies in Japan whose primary function is engaging in international business, and a significant percentage of the country's major manufacturers have their own export departments. But the fact remains that the Japanese do not conduct very much of their business through written correspondence. Their system gives precedence to and often makes mandatory the face-to-face meeting and the development of a personal relationship before any business transpires.

Yakusoku
"On My Word"

Japanese businessmen generally do all they can to avoid getting involved with the law and the courts. In the past, it was customary in Japan for both parties in a dispute to be regarded as equally guilty. "Justice" was often both harsh and expensive, and under any circumstances it was usually wise to avoid bringing oneself to the attention of the authorities.

In Japan today the law is still regarded as a costly and complicated process. The American tendency to bring in lawyers on business negotiations and to drawn up minutely detailed contracts can be very upsetting to the Japanese. They prefer general agreements that allow the parties to discuss and negotiate particular points as they come up, leaving both sides a great deal more flexibility.

The Japanese businessman's credo is that every effort should be made to avoid problems by cooperating on an individual and personal, as well as company and industry, level; and when problems do arise, they should be solved by arbitration and compromise. Their view is that since it is impossible to know exactly what is going to happen in the future, detailed, written contracts are bound to become outdated in just a short time.

In the past, there were few written contracts in Japan. They depended instead on *yakusoku* (yah-kuu-soe-kuu), "verbal agreements," with the parties bound to each other by goodwill and obligation. When such agreements were reached and were of some importance, they were usually marked by a drinking party and the ceremonial clapping of hands a prescribed number of times in a particular cadence.

While disliking and distrusting written contracts, Japanese businessmen recognize that they have little or no choice but to use them in their international business. They are especially sensitive to the fact that they usually do not know their foreign "partners" very well, cannot *amaeru* with them in full confidence and trust, and cannot depend on dealing with the same individuals from one day to the next, much less from year to year.

Sekinin Sha
Finding Where the Buck Stops

In Western countries there is almost always one person who has final authority and responsibility, and it is easy to identify this person. All you have to do is ask, "Who is in charge?" In Japanese companies, however, no one individual is in charge. Both authority and responsibility are dispersed among the managers as a group. The larger the company, the more people are involved. When there are mistakes or failures, Japanese management does not try to single out any individual to blame. They try to focus on the cause of the failing in an effort to find out why it happened. In this way, the employee who made the mistake (if one individual was involved) does not lose face, and all concerned have an opportunity to learn a lesson.

Ranking Japanese businessmen advise that it is difficult to determine who has real authority and who makes final decisions in a Japanese company. Said a Sony director: "Even a top executive must consult his colleagues before he 'makes' a decision because he has become a high executive more by his seniority than his leadership ability. To keep harmony in his company he must act as a member of a family." Sony's co-founder Akio Morita adds that because of this factor, the traditional concept of promotion by seniority may not have much of a future in Japan. He agrees, however, that it is not something that can be changed in a short period of time.

In approaching a Japanese company about a business matter, it is therefore almost always necessary to meet and talk with the heads of several sections and departments on different occasions. After having gone through this procedure, you may still not get a clear-cut response from anyone, particularly if the various managers you approached have not come to a favorable consensus among themselves. It is often left up to you to synthesize the individual responses you receive and draw your own conclusions.

It is always important and often absolutely essential that the outsider (foreign or Japanese) starting a new business relationship with a Japanese company establish good rapport with each level of management in the company. Only by doing so can the outsider be sure his side of the story, his needs and expectations, will get across to all the necessary management levels.

Earle Okumura, a Los Angeles-based consultant, and one of the few Americans who is bilingual and bicultural and has had extensive business experience in Japan, suggests the following approach to establishing "lines of communication" with a Japanese company when the project concerns the introductions of new technology to be used by the Japanese firm:

Step I—Ask a director or the head of the Research & Development Department to introduce you to the *kacho* (section chief) who is going to be directly in charge of your project within his department. Take the time to develop a personal relationship with the *kacho* (eating and drinking with him, etc.) then ask him to tell you exactly what you should do, and how you should go about trying to achieve and maintain the best possible working relationship with the company.

Step II—Ask the R&D *kacho*, with whom you now have at least the beginning of an *amae* relationship, to introduce you to his counterparts in the Production Department, Quality Control, and Sales Departments, etc., and go through the same get-acquainted process with each of them, telling them about yourself, your company, and your responsibilities. In all of these contacts, care must be taken not to pose any kind of threat or embarrassment to the different section managers.

Step III—After you have established a good, working relationship with the various *kacho* concerned, thoroughly explained your side of the project, and gained an understanding of their thinking, responsibilities, and capabilities, the third step is to get an appointment with the managing director or president of the company for a relaxed, casual conversation about policies, how much you appreciate being able to work with his company, and the advantages that should accrue to both parties as a result of the joint venture.

Do not, Okumura cautions, get involved in trying to pursue details of the project with the managing director or president. He will most likely not be familiar with them and, in any event, will be more concerned about your reliability, sincerity, and ability to deal with the company.

Before an American businessman commits himself to doing business with another company, he checks out the company's assets, technology, financial stability, etc. The Japanese businessman is first interested in the character and quality of the people in the other company and secondarily interested in its facilities and finances. The Japanese put more stock in goodwill and the quality of interpersonal relationships in their business dealings.

Mizu Shobai
The "Water Business"

Mizu shobai (Mee-zoo show-bye), literally "water business," is a euphemism for the so-called entertainment trade—which is another euphemism for the hundreds of thousands of bars, cabarets, night clubs, "soap houses" (formerly known as Turkish baths), hotspring spas, and geisha inns that flourish in Japan. The term *mizu* is applied to this area of Japanese life because, like pleasure, water sparkles and soothes, then goes down the drain or evaporates into the air (and the business of catering to fleshly pleasures was traditionally associated with hot baths). *Shobai* or "business" is a very appropriate word, because the *mizu shobai* is one of the biggest businesses in Japan, employing some five million men and women.*

Drinking and enjoying the companionship of attractive young women in *mizu shobai* establishments is an important part of the lives of Japanese businessmen. There are basically two reasons for their regular drinking. First, ritualistic drinking developed into an integral part of religious life in ancient times, and from there it was carried over into social and business life.

Thus, for centuries, no formal function or business dealing of any kind has been complete without a drinking party *(uchiage)* (uu-chee-ah-gay) to mark the occasion. At such times, drinking is more of a duty than anything else. Only a person who cannot drink because of some physical condition or illness is normally excused.

The second reason for the volume of customary drinking that goes on in Japan is related to the distinctive subordinate-superior relationships between people and to the minutely prescribed etiquette that prevents the Japanese from being completely informal and frank with each other *except when drinking.*

---

*For more about the subject of *mizu shobai*, see the author's *Bachelor's Japan.*

Because the Japanese must be so circumspect in their behavior at all "normal" times, they believe it is impossible to
really get to know a person without drinking with him. The
sober person, they say, will always hold back and not reveal
his true character. They feel ill at ease with anyone who refuses to drink with them at a party or outing. They feel that
refusing to drink indicates a person is arrogant, excessively
proud, and unfriendly. The ultimate expression of goodwill,
trust, and humility is to drink to drunkenness with your co-
workers and with close or important business associates in
general. Those who choose for any reason not to go all the
way must simulate drunkenness in order to fulfill the requirements of the custom.

Enjoying the companionship of pretty, young women has
long been a universal prerogative of successful men everywhere. In Japan it often goes further than that. It has traditionally been used as an inducement to engage in business as
well as to seal bargains, probably because it is regarded as the
most intimate activity men can share.

When the Japanese businessman offers his Western guest
or client intimate access to the charms of attractive and willing
young women—something that still happens regularly—he is
not "pandering" or engaging in any other "nasty" practice.
He is merely offering the Western businessman a form of
hospitality that has been popular in Japan since ancient times.
In short, Japanese businessmen do openly and without guilt
feelings, what many Western businessmen do furtively.

The foreign businessman who "passes" when offered the
opportunity to indulge in this honorable Japanese custom,
either before or after a bargain is struck, may be regarded as
foolish or prudish for letting the opportunity go by, but he is
no longer likely to be accused of insincerity.

Many Westerners find it difficult to join in wholeheartedly
at the round of parties typically held for them by their Japanese hosts, especially if it is nothing more than a drinking
party at a bar or cabaret. Westerners have been conditioned
to intersperse their drinking with jokes, boasting, and long-
winded opinions—supposedly rational—on religion, politics,
business, or what-have-you.

Japanese businessmen, on the other hand, do not go to bars

or clubs at night to have serious discussions. They go there to relax emotionally and physically—to let it all hang out. They joke, laugh, sing, dance, and make short, rapid-fire comments about work, their superiors, personal problems, and so on; but they do not have long, deep discussions.

When the otherwise reserved and carefully controlled Japanese businessman does relax in a bar, cabaret, or at a drinking party, he often acts—from a Western viewpoint—like a high school kid in his "cups" for the first time.

At a reception given by a group of American dignitaries at one of Tokyo's leading hotels, my table partner was the chief of the research division of the Japanese company being honored. The normally sober and distinguished scientist had had a few too many by the time the speeches began, and he was soon acting in the characteristic manner of the Japanese drunk. All during the speeches he giggled, sang, burped, and whooped it up, much to the embarrassment of both sides.

Most Japanese businessmen, particularly those in lower and middle management, drink regularly and have developed an extraordinary capacity to drink heavily night after night and keep up their day-to-day work. Since they drink to loosen up and enjoy themselves, to be hospitable and to get to know their drinking partners, they are suspicious of anyone who drinks and remains formal and sober. They call this "killing the sake," with the added connotation that it also kills the pleasure.

During a boisterous drinking bout in which they sing and dance and trade risqué banter with hostesses or geisha, Japanese businessmen often sober up just long enough to have an important business exchange with a guest or colleague and then go back to the fun and games.

Foreign businessmen should be very cautious about trying to keep up with their Japanese hosts at such drinking rituals. It is all too common to see visiting businessmen being returned to their hotels well after midnight, sodden drunk. The key to this important ceremony is to drink moderately and simulate drunkenness.

In recent years, inflation has dimmed some of the nightly glow from geisha houses, the great cabarets, the bars, and the "in" restaurants in Japan's major cities. The feeling is also growing that the several billion dollars spent each year in the *mizu shobai* is incompatible with Japan's present-day needs. But like so many other aspects of Japanese life, the *mizu shobai* is deeply embedded in the overall socioeconomic system, as well as in the national psyche. It is not about to disappear in the foreseeable future.

Most of the money spent in the *mizu shobai* comes from the so-called *Sha-Yo Zoku* (Shah-Yoe Zoe-kuu), "Expense-Account Tribe"—the large number of salesmen, managers, and executives who are authorized to entertain clients, prospects, and guests at company expense. Japanese companies are permitted a substantial tax write-off for entertainment expenses to begin with, and most go way beyond the legal limit (based on their capital), according to both official and unofficial sources.

6

Nippongo
The Magnificent Barrier

Japlish
Smooth as a Baby's Ass

Some years ago, one of Japan's Big Three newspapers, with a circulation of over five million, carried an advertisement that was all in Japanese except for the headline. The headline read: "SMOOTH AS A BABY'S ASS."

The advertisement was indicative of a language/communications problem (the obsession to use English whether appropriate or not) that is apparently unique among the world's leading nations. Since every language is a mirror of the culture in which it was developed, it is not surprising that the Japanese language reflects the psychology, attitudes, and manners of the Japanese. In fact, as mentioned earlier, the Japanese language is the primary repository and transmitter of Japanese culture.

Japanese was a relatively adequate language as long as the Japanese dealt only with themselves and were able to maintain the character and style of their unique social system. Neither of these two conditions has existed for some time now, but the awkward tongue and centuries of machinelike conditioning still shackle the Japanese to their heritage.

There are three basic levels of the Japanese language: the "low" level used when addressing subordinates and some categories of younger persons; the "intimate" level used when

98

conversing with family members and close friends of the same age; and an honorific or "high" level used when addressing superiors and respected elders, or when being conspicuously polite to someone for any reason. There is also a fourth category of Japanese, one that is used in newspapers and consists of a condensed, telegraphic style that expresses only the key thoughts and leaves the reader to fill in the rest.

Japanese etiquette demands that the proper level of language be used for every situation, and, of course, using either the common or low level of language to a superior is the worst possible breach of this deeply embedded social rule.

The trilevel character of the Japanese language, which grew out of the vertically structured social system, is one of the reasons why it is so difficult for the Japanese to talk to strangers. Until they find out the other person's social/business rank, they are very ill at ease. The Japanese can, in fact, approach and talk to foreigners easier than they can talk to another Japanese if they know a foreign language, because they do not have to be concerned about the social level of the language they use.

The Japanese language thus owes its most distinctive characteristics to the fact that those using it must take the most extreme care not to insult or shame anyone. This also partly explains the remarkably polite manners of the Japanese in all their normal social contacts with each other (and in most cases with foreigners)—discounting boarding crowded subways and trains, shopping in department stores, etc., as "normal" contact.

Both the language and etiquette, inseparably intertwined, are a reflection of the inherent desire of the Japanese to obviate shame-causing situations, or to prevent insults. The language is almost bare of curse words. The speaker who wants to flay someone has to depend upon manner of delivery rather than word meaning. The only "curse" words that do exist are regularly heard on radio and television. Children playing in the streets hurl them at one another and at adult passersby with complete abandon and without fear of being overly censored by their elders.

Once a Japanese has been shamed by the deliberate misuse of language, whether or not he deserves the shame, he will

react along perfectly predictable lines. He will become in-
censed and seek revenge which he must have if it takes the
rest of his life. Or, if there is no possible way he can get back at
the one who shamed him, he will become morbidly depressed
and somehow inflict punishment on himself.

There are many Japanese today who are able to stand up
under verbal insults—for example, young people, salesmen,
and women in the entertainment trades. Others are also
gradually discovering that they can escape the web that binds
them to "The Japanese Way." But their numbers are still
relatively small. There are stories regularly in the daily newspapers recounting incidents of someone taking revenge—on
someone else or himself—for being verbally shamed.

Very few foreigners, including long-time residents of Japan, speak Japanese. The vast majority of the Japanese speak
little or no English (or any other foreign language). The
language barrier, coupled with other cultural differences relating to communication, causes more of the problems that
beset Japanese and Westerners doing business with one another than any other factor.

To give credit where it is due, hundreds of thousands of
Japanese, particularly those going into international business, at least make an attempt to learn English. Most Western
businessmen, however, especially high-placed ones, consider
learning Japanese too time-consuming, unnecessary, or beneath their dignity. Some who have been in Japan for decades
exhibit a perverse pride in their inability to speak the language, and they regularly insult Japanese who fail to understand their comments or questions.

Almost all Japanese study English from two to eight years,
and many of them will list English as something they have
"accomplished." But only a tiny percentage of the population
can converse even halfway fluently in the language or understand it when it is spoken to them. The reason for this is that
their teachers in school could not speak English and therefore could not teach it as a spoken language. While a tremendous amount of effort is expended in "reading" English, it is
read without benefit of knowing how to pronounce it. It thus
comes out "Japanized."

The English word *bread* becomes "bu-re-do" when spoken

or read by most Japanese. Similarly, *coming* becomes "ko-mi-n-gu"; *Mr. Smith* becomes "Mi-su-ta Su-mi-su"; *girl* becomes "ga-ru"; and so on.

The English that students are required by their teachers to study is often truly astounding. Innumerable times students have come to me and asked for help in translating an ordinary assignment. The selections they had been given were so esoteric, so stream of consciousness and vague, not one in a hundred native-born English speakers could have explained them in their own tongue!

Some of the wilder examples would shock the Western student if he should be called upon to render them into a foreign tongue. Here is one of my favorites, quoted by Anthony Scarangello in his book, *A Fulbright Teacher in Japan**:

> The march of mankind is directed neither by his will, nor by his superstitions, but by the effect of his great and, as it were, accidental discoveries on his average nature. The discovery and exploitation of fire, of metals and gunpowder, of coal, steam, electricity, of flying machines, acting on human nature which is, practically speaking, constant, molds the real shape of human life, under all the agreeable camouflage of religions, principles, policies and ideas. The comparisons with the effect of these discoveries and their unconscious influences on human life, the effect of political ideas is seen to be inconsiderable.

Haji
Avoiding Shame

The difficulty of learning English is further complicated by a supersensitive pride that often prevents the Japanese, once they attain professional status, from either admitting that their English is less than fluent or seeking help from someone who does know the language to advise them or proofread their publications, signs, etc., that are supposed to be in English.

---

*Anthony Scarangello, *A Fulbright Teacher in Japan* (Tokyo: The Hokuseido Press, 1957), p. 123.

The answer to this paradox seems to be that as long as no one points out the errors to the people responsible, it is possible for them to assume there are no errors, so no "face" is lost. And it is considered extremely impolite for anyone to point out such mistakes. Before I became aware of such protocol, I often seriously embarrassed Japanese friends, co-workers, and government bureaucrats by calling attention to flagrant and harmful errors in everything from menus to white papers issued by one of the ministries.

Larger Japanese firms generally have a number of employees who speak English quite well. Other firms usually have at least one or two who speak broken English and, with the aid of a dictionary, can laboriously turn out letters in the language and can translate English-language correspondence into Japanese.

These latter firms may never completely understand all the things foreign businessmen say or write to them, and as a result they are almost always working in some degree of darkness. Even when information or instructions are given to a Japanese company in Japanese, the possibility of a misunderstanding or failure to get through is enormous.

Because of both the inherent vagueness of the Japanese language and the distinctive attitudes and social behavior that continue to force the Japanese to use their language in a vague, esoteric manner, even well-educated, erudite people often have difficulty expressing themselves clearly. A Tokyo University professor whose specialty is communications estimates that on the first time around the Japanese fully understand only about eighty-five percent of what they say to one another.

It is common for Japanese to have to repeat themselves several times to get across relatively simple concepts. The language is so vague that in many ordinary conversations people frequently have to stop and trace one or more Chinese ideograms—usually with their finger on any handy surface or in the air—in order to communicate an idea. If the ideogram happens to be an unusual one (there are hundreds of unusual ones) or if a person has either forgotten or never learned it, he may never fully understand.

The Japanese language actually can be spoken much more

directly and much more effectively than it is by most Japanese, but for a Japanese to do so is regarded as a serious breach of etiquette. Foreigners who have a good command of the language are often able to communicate ideas more quickly and clearly than the Japanese, since they are not forced by habit or Japanese propriety to speak in esoteric circumlocutions. In doing so, however, they run the risk of seriously offending whomever they are talking to, so it is necessary for them to exercise caution.

Sukoshi Dekimasu
I Can Do a Little

A smattering of Japanese is easy to learn and will prevent many of the situations which cause basic problems for the foreigner in Japan. These usually are concerned with simple things like food, lodging, time, direction, etc., and require only a small vocabulary and little or no knowledge of grammar. A great many of the more common problems of communication occur in the first place because the foreigner tends to assume automatically that any Japanese person he encounters will understand English.

I have watched visiting travelers and businessmen approach Japanese clerks, office personnel, policemen, and others with questions, sometimes simple and sometimes complicated—as if it would be the most natural thing in the world for them to understand English—and then be unbecomingly indignant when it turned out that they didn't.

Most Westerners who have studied a foreign language can understand more than they can speak. In Japan it is usually just the opposite. The typical Japanese who has studied the language can generally say many things in English, if given the time to laboriously string the words together. This misleads foreigners into believing that everything they say is understood, and so they ramble on and on and are sorely disappointed when the Japanese person fails to react as expected.

It seems to be customary for some foreigners to assume that raising their voices and becoming angry will help them communicate with Japanese whose understanding of English is limited. They eventually find, however, that this does not achieve the desired results. It serves only to further befuddle the Japanese, and it turns them into enemies who will never forget nor forgive and one day, in some way, will take their revenge.

In many cases, it is difficult to determine immediately how much English an individual speaks or understands. The visiting businessman or traveler can avoid some of the complications that frequently arise in such situations by engaging the individual concerned in a bit of preliminary conversation to see how much he or she understands. If the topic is important and if the person's understanding seems doubtful, the best thing to do is write out what you have to say.

Foreign businessmen who receive letters from Japanese firms written in adequate English are also cautioned to remember that there is an excellent chance that their answering letter will not be thoroughly understood. This is not always because of inability on the part of the Japanese. I have examined more than a thousand letters from foreign firms to Japanese companies and found some of them completely incomprehensible. Many others were so general or so cryptic that much of the meaning was obscured.

Besides a language barrier that makes communication between Japanese and Westerners difficult, there are other cultural factors that hinder the Japanese in their relations with outsiders. For many centuries the Japanese were taught to repress their emotions in public; to display no curiosity, surprise, displeasure, or pain in the presence of a superior; and to obey all orders without question.

Still today in the educational system in Japan, there is very little student participation and there is little or no discussion in most classes. The teacher lectures; the students listen and take notes. One of the results of this system is that the average Japanese has a difficult time responding quickly to blunt questions and also finds it hard to express feelings verbally with anywhere near the amount of freedom and enthusiasm expected by Americans, for example.

The Japanese are well aware that their language is difficult; they know it has its limitations as an effective means of communication. At the same time they have traditionally regarded their unique language as an important line of defense against foreign intrusion, spying, or snooping, not only in the political and diplomatic spheres but also in economic and social activities.

Wakarimasu Ka?
Getting Through

Over the generations, so few Westerners have mastered the Japanese language that the Japanese came to believe that it couldn't be learned by Europeans and that its impenetrability provided them with a protective cloak of inestimable value. As a result of this attitude, the Japanese have always been more than willing to at least try to learn foreign languages, and they continue to be amazed, even shocked, when confronted by a foreigner who speaks their language.

The Japanese also continue to be extraordinarily sensitive to racial differences. To hear their own language coming out of a foreigner's mouth, especially when the foreigner is caucasian or black, is a surprise that often has rather startling consequences. The image of Japanese-speaking foreigners is so remote from their minds, it often happens that a Westerner will say something in fluent Japanese and fail to be understood—because the Japanese are not mentally tuned to "receive" in their own language.

A Western lawyer who conducts cases in Japanese once walked up to a policeman in downtown Tokyo and asked him in Japanese if he knew the whereabouts of an address in the area. The policeman looked uncomfortable for several seconds, then blurted out, "I no speak English!" This peeved the lawyer and he proceeded to lecture the unfortunate cop in such a loud voice that a crowd gathered.

The lawyer could probably have saved himself a lot of bother and the police officer a lot of embarrassment if he had remembered to preface his question with one of the several conversational openers which the Japanese customarily use and which, when a foreigner is concerned, serve to let the Japanese know that you are going to speak in Japanese and that they should prepare to receive in their own language.

If one knows how to bow properly, it is often possible to bow and get the same message across. But this takes more skill and experience than might be expected. The most effective method is to combine a bow with one of the commonly used polite prefaces. On occasion this doesn't work either, so there is no choice but to repeat yourself.

The linguistic weaknesses of the Japanese—coupled with their characteristic reluctance to admit to this weakness—is, of course, responsible for the strange and sometimes hilarious English-language advertising they do, especially when the ads are prepared by their own in-house advertising departments.

Tsuyaku
"Thinking," Not Just Words

Foreign businessmen have often related how they spent hour after hour trying to convey something important (to them) to their Japanese counterparts, only to find their efforts wasted and the Japanese probably thinking they were "blithering idiots." One such American recently recounting an experience along this line, summed up the crux of the problem very aptly when he described the kind of interpreter that is needed when talking or negotiating with Japanese businessmen. He said, "You need someone who can interpret thinking, not just words."

This same businessman also brought out another facet of Japanese social and business etiquette that often contributes to misunderstandings, friction, and delays in Japanese-Western business relations. In his case, he had as an interpreter a young Japanese who had lived for many years in the United States and was quite fluent in English. Believing that having such a qualified interpreter gave him an opportunity to get all of his ideas across to his Japanese counterpart, he spent a number of hours carefully and precisely explaining his whole business philosophy, how he felt that their business could and should be operated.

When he returned to his hotel he was thoroughly satisfied

that he had finally penetrated the language barrier. But he congratulated himself too soon. Shortly afterward he received a phone call from the interpreter who apologized, saying he had not translated most of the foreign businessman's comments because they would have "offended" the Japanese. The Western businessman's remarks, it seems, were mostly critical of the way the Japanese do business.

It is a serious breach of etiquette in Japan to criticize someone directly in public, even when the relationship is superior-to-subordinate; just as it has traditionally been "wrong" to disagree with people in public or to be right when they are in error.

This social custom often forces intelligent people to appear foolish or stupid or indifferent, but it is an important means of avoiding behavior that others, both in inferior and superior positions, consider insulting. There are historical examples in Japan of people who forfeited their lives by publicly correcting or criticizing someone. Revenge for this type of insult today usually does not involve violence (except sometimes in the case of hoodlums), but it is often vicious in a subtle way. The Western businessman should be aware of this extraordinary sensitivity of the Japanese and conduct himself accordingly.

One way of reducing possible friction in this area is for Western businessmen to explain that besides being unfamiliar with Japanese customs, the policies and practices of his own company which he cannot arbitrarily change make it impossible for him to conform completely to "the Japanese Way." This is something like announcing to the Japanese, "I may insult you but I can't help it, and I apologize beforehand"— reasoning that is readily understood in Japan.

A vital factor in the use of English-speaking Japanese interpreters by foreign businessmen in Japan is that most of the interpreters are young, often have had little or no business experience themselves, are likely to be inadequately experienced in handling human relations problems (which is always a big part of interpreting), and are almost always called upon to interpret to older, higher ranking Japanese executives.

In their efforts to use the proper level of polite speech to

higher ranking individuals, the young, inexperienced interpreters often confuse the meaning of what they are trying to
say. They will also habitually "water down" the foreigner's
remarks to avoid upsetting the Japanese side.

Because of such problems, it is usually wiser for the foreign
businessman to employ older persons as interpreters—even
when their English-language proficiency may be less than
that of a recent university graduate (who may have studied
abroad). The greater social status of the older individual will
often more than compensate for a lesser ability in English.

If the foreign businessman wants to further balance the
scales in his favor by engaging the services of an older man of
recognized social and economic rank, he should explain to
the man of rank that his high status, knowledge, and experience are needed to offset the foreigner's lack of understanding of local customs, etc.

Gaijin Kusai
Smelling Like a Foreigner

Foreign businessmen commonly assume that a Western-educated Japanese employee, interpreter, friend, or contact who
speaks adequate if not fluent English is a "friend" in an "enemy camp" who can be depended upon to carry out their
orders and wishes fully. While each case has to be considered
individually, this is generally not so. There are a number of
interesting reasons why it is not so.

First and most important, if the Western-educated Japanese is in a medium-sized or larger organization, and especially if he is not one of the top executives, he is up against a
system that constitutes the very soul of the Japanese, and
despite his foreign veneer he is still very much a part of that
system.

The Japanese are inexpressibly sensitive and proud, and if
a co-worker should appear to flaunt his Western learning
gained by actually living in the outside world, he takes the
chance of being ostracized and forever relegated to the background in some meaningless position.

Over the years I have seen how difficult it is for Japanese

who have studied overseas to get themselves back into the system and maintain friendly relations with their Japanese co-workers. They must exercise extreme care not to arouse the jealousy or ire of their fellow employees. Companies, of course, send their own employees abroad, but not until they have been fully indoctrinated in the company spirit and philosophy.

Many major Japanese companies still today have a more or less set policy against hiring anyone who has studied abroad. Their attitude is based on the sure knowledge that the individual who studies abroad invariably loses some of his Japaneseness and takes on what to "pure" Japanese are very noticeable Western attitudes and manners, thereby becoming a square peg in a round hole—even though "better qualified" than other members of the firm. In earlier years, such returned students were often described as *gaijin kusai* (guy-jeen kuu-sie), "smelling like a foreigner."

During the years I lived in Tokyo, I interviewed dozens of Japanese in their middle and late twenties who had studied overseas for extended periods and could not get jobs with major Japanese companies because they happened to be without very powerful personal connections. Others I know of who were able to get jobs had to be content with positions in which their abilities, especially in English, were not used.

The companies concerned prefer to continue using Japanese employees who have studied only in Japan, even though they are capable only of writing and speaking a sort of pidgin English. They explain the policy by claiming that the Japanese who become Westernized are no longer emotionally or intellectually capable of fitting into the unique Japanese system. Since it is absolutely necessary for many Japanese firms to have employees who can read, write, and speak foreign languages well, some companies do make the "sacrifice" and employ people who have studied overseas.

The foreign-educated Japanese employee thus tends to become a buffer between foreigners and his firm. When he speaks to the foreigner, he puts on his Western veneer and understands and sympathizes with the foreigner. When he turns around and speaks to his Japanese colleagues and seniors, the system demands that he become one of them and do his best to see the foreigner through Japanese eyes.

When a number of Japanese companies with extensive international operations announced in late 1985 that they would thereafter annually hire a number of Japanese graduates of foreign universities for assignment in their overseas branches, it was such a break from the norm that it made the national news.

Makoto
Sincerity, Japanese Style

It is not unusual for both Japanese and Western businessmen to accuse each other of being insincere—and sometimes dishonest. What neither side appreciates is that in most cases they are referring to entirely different concepts of sincerity and honesty. In many situations, the Japanese idea of right and wrong is quite different from the Western idea. To the typical Japanese, right or wrong is not so much based on an unvarying, universal code of ethics or principles as it is upon time, place, the people involved, and other circumstances. The Japanese concept of justice is subsequently not as abstract as the Western idea.

I once attended a large reception staged in Tokyo by the importing division of an American company for Hitachi Ltd., one of their suppliers, and several guests of note. There were a number of speeches by Hitachi executives, and in every case the speaker not only began and ended his talk with an appeal for the Americans to be sincere in their dealings with them but also harped on this point throughout his speech.

Catching the spirit of the thing, some of the American speakers countered and asked the Japanese to also be sincere, in what an outsider would probably have thought were spontaneous demonstrations of goodwill in which both parties were talking about the same thing and were really communicating with one another. But sincerity as used by the Japanese has altogether a different meaning than it does to Westerners. And it is of course vitally important to understand this difference when doing business with Japanese.

Sincerity to most Westerners means free from pretense or

deceit. In other words, honest and truthful without reserva-
tions. But to the typical Japanese, being *makoto* (mah-koe-toe)
means to properly discharge all of one's obligations so that
everything will flow smoothly; so that harmony will be maintained. It also means being careful not to say or do anything
that would cause loss of face. By extension, it further means
that the *makoto* person will not be self-seeking, will not get
excited or provoke others to excitement, will not reveal his
innermost thoughts if they are negative, will not, in fact, do
anything disruptive.

This, obviously, does not necessarily include or require
strict adherence to what Westerners like to call "honesty" and
"frankness," since harmony of a kind can be maintained in-
definitely as long as both sides play according to the same
rules. And the Japanese, just like the Westerners, tend to
think and behave as if their rules were the ones being used.

The Japanese businessman, as mentioned earlier, often
seems to be more concerned with form and manner than he
is with the end results of any effort—although results are, of
course, important to him. Since this attitude is nearly opposite typical Western thinking, it naturally causes varying degrees of misunderstanding and friction between the parties
involved.

Japanese still tend to think in terms of personal relationships and subjective circumstances in their business dealings.
Thus an agreement between a Japanese and a foreign businessman should be reduced to its basic elements, and each
point should be thoroughly discussed to make sure each side
understands and actually agrees to what the other side is
saying.

But reaching an agreement with a Japanese company does
not mean the foreign company is home free. From the instant
the agreement is made or signed, the interests of the two
parties will begin to diverge. The agreement will be interpreted differently by the two sides, and unless there is ongoing
"root binding" and nurturing of the agreement by face-to-
face dialogue and adjustments, the interests of the two parties
are likely to be so far apart within two or three years that the
relationship goes sour.

This usually happens not because of dishonesty or devious-ness on the part of either party, but simply because of differences in the perceptions and reactions of the two parties. Among other things, it is the Japanese position that since circumstances change regularly, it is natural that contractual relationships between companies also change regularly.

One of the major weaknesses of American businessmen dealing with Japan, particularly in joint ventures, is their failure to recognize and react positively to the constant need to nurture and adjust their relationships with their Japanese partners.

7

Yamato Damashii
The Spirit of Japan

Ware Ware Nippon-Jin
"We Japanese"

For centuries the Japanese have referred to their distinctive spirit and character as *Yamato Damashii* (Yah-mah-toe Dah-mah-shee). *Yamato* is written with ideograms that mean "Great Peace," and is the old word for Japan. *Damashii* means "heart" or "soul." Put together, they refer to the traditional spirit and personality of the Japanese in much the same way that "Puritan ethic" is sometimes used in reference to characteristics of certain categories of Americans.

The use of the word *Yamato* in this context is significant because it emphasizes the traditional Japanese preoccupation with peace and harmony. Of course, this is "Japanese" peace and harmony, according to their values and definitions, and as expressed in the key words already discussed: *amae, on, giri, tsukiai,* etc. There are other important words and phrases that elaborate the nuances of Japanese values, feelings, fears, and aspirations.

Jibun Ga Nai
Life without a "Self"

The Japanese, in particular those born before the 1950s, tend to have shallow and fragile concepts of themselves as individual entities. There is a phrase used to express this feeling, *jibun ga nai* (jee-boon gah nie), "I have no self," which sociologists say is probably unique to the Japanese.

It is not difficult, of course, to understand why this feeling became an important aspect of the Japanese character. The traditional "Japanese Way" gave precedence in all things to the family and the group. Also, in virtually all instances, status and function were more important than the individual.

Just one of the ways this factor affects the foreign businessman in Japan or in dealings with Japanese is graphically illustrated by a typical incident that took place recently. A foreign businessman took his two top Japanese assistants to the United States for a familiarization tour of his company's American operations. The Japanese executives had been with the Japan branch of the U.S. company for several years and, of course, knew the American resident director very well.

During all the years the two Japanese managers had worked with the American businessman in Tokyo, they had never once called him by his first name. It was always "Mr. So-and-so." Within a day after the three men arrived in the U.S., however, the Japanese were calling their American employer by his given name in an atmosphere of intimate friendliness and rapport that is so characteristic of American behavior.

"I thought," said the American businessman, "that we had finally achieved a breakthrough in our relations—and that we would thereafter be on a much more satisfying level in both our business and personal relationships.

"But," he added, "much to my surprise and disappointment, no sooner were we back in Japan than those two fine gentlemen dropped the relaxed relationship we had developed while in the U.S., became rather stiff in their manners and began again calling me by my last name."

This incident emphasizes an extraordinary dilemma in Japanese society today. After centuries of repressing their emotions, their desires, and even their spirits for the sake of harmony in a meticulously prescribed hierarchically ranked social system, the Japanese lost much of the ability to exercise their own individuality.

This system of deemphasizing the individual in favor of the group was further strengthened by giving the name of the clan, the place of residence, and the occupation and title precedence over the individual's name.

Still today the use of the given name is rare among adults in Japan. In business and the professions, the identity of the individual is usually blurred—and in some cases made virtually nonexistent.

The individual becomes obscured somewhere in the shadows of his position or occupation and is addressed by his title or function instead of his name. The president of a company is addressed as "President" *(Shacho)*. Department heads are addressed as "Department Head" *(Bucho)*. Teachers are addressed as "Teacher" or "Professor" *(Sensei)*. The butcher is addressed as "Mr. Meatman" *(Nikuya-san)*, and so on, resulting in one of the most inhibiting, limiting, and painful personal handicaps now facing the Japanese.

Having lived and worked in Japan for many years, I can personally testify to the damage this system does to the relationships between Japanese and non-Japanese, especially Americans who have a profound need for such intimacy.

I have had close relationships with many Japanese for more than thirty years, but there is still a deep psychological barrier that prevents me from feeling perfectly at ease with them *because I have to call them Mr. Yamaguchi, Mr. Kameda, or Mr. Sato!*

It may be hard to believe that this barrier can be so powerful, so disturbing; but it is and it has a pervasive influence on Japan's business relationships with the rest of the world.

This barrier to intimacy does not exist just between Japanese and foreigners. It also exists between Japanese; and the pain, frustration, longing, and loneliness it causes appears to be even more acute. The Japanese are aware of the baleful influence of this outmoded, feudalistic, and inhuman system; nevertheless, it is so deeply rooted in their society that they have so far found it impossible to discard.

It is my belief that until the Japanese can succeed in eliminating this aspect of their system and establishing their own personal identities by calling each other—as well as non-Japanese—by their given names, they will continue to suffer poignant feelings of inadequacy and insecurity and will be at a serious disadvantage in their efforts to become full-fledged members of the world community.

Younger Japanese, and the older Japanese who have managed to become more individualistic in their attitudes and actions, are not nearly as "nameless" as the typical Japanese adult, but they are severely restricted in their relationships with others, especially with other Japanese. It is difficult for them to react spontaneously and frankly to outsiders, especially non-Japanese, although it is true that in almost every case not connected with business they make a genuine and generous effort.

Risshin Shusse
The Japanese Success Drive

The extraordinary diligence and ambition of the Japanese is world famous. What is not so well known is exactly why the Japanese are so success oriented. The mainspring of the seemingly frenetic drive of the Japanese—which sprang into full bloom virtually overnight when Japan's feudal Shogunate government was replaced in 1868—is apparently a combination of several historical factors, including their self-image as a superior people and the fact that ambition among common people was for the most part sternly suppressed from earliest times to the beginning of the modern industrial era.

During Japan's long Feudal Age (1192-1868), social class and occupations were generally hereditary. The only characteristics that were approved and rewarded were dedication to hard work and loyalty to superiors within the rigid family, clan, and Shogun system.

With the fall of the feudal system in 1868, the new government began an intensive campaign to bring the country up to the industrial level of the United States and the advanced European nations. Part of this campaign was an intense effort to imbue every child in the country with a concept of success known as *Risshin shusse*, (Rees-sheen shus-say), or something like "Rise to eminence (in the world) through success!"

"*Shusse* success is distinctive in that it places major emphasis on the group instead of the individual," explains Hiroshi Hazama, professor of Industrial Sociology at the Tokyo University of Education. The success of the individual depends on the success of the group, beginning with the immediate work group, and by extension going all the way up to include the whole country.

Professor Hazama adds that *shusse* success is not measured in terms of wealth, but in social position. Social status is achieved by becoming a teacher, doctor, or businessman. The apex of social status is to become the leader of one's group, regardless of its size, and to receive the coveted title of *cho*. This title, with its accompanying social prestige rather than conspicuous financial rewards, is the criterion of *shusse* success. Of course, the purity of this motive has suffered considerably in recent dates, since currently life-styles in Japan make financial success an absolute necessity.

Hazama adds that the social status gained from being an employer is also of vital importance in the Japanese value system—a factor that contributes to the penchant of the Japanese to form their own companies, no matter how small or precarious.

Defeat in World War II had a profound effect on the attitudes of the Japanese toward success. The family system in which the father or ranking male member was the absolute master was abolished. The introduction of "American-style" democracy made everyone equal in the eyes of the law. Wartime destruction reduced the overwhelming majority to the same economic level—flat-out poverty.

These new postwar conditions led to the rapid replacement of the *shusse* or family-group concept of success by that of personal success in terms of both social position and the accumulation of wealth. Titles were still of vital importance, but so was money. Besides the compulsion of the formerly affluent to regain their lost wealth, those who had never before known anything except subsistence-level existence were free for the first time to better themselves. Their compulsion to overcome the shame of their defeat in war and the energy provided by their new personal freedom were channeled into an overriding ambition to raise their economic and social levels.

Ki Ga Susumanai
120 Million Dissatisfied Spirits

Psychiatrist Takeo Doi says that the renowned industrious-
ness of the Japanese cannot be fully explained without reference to a condition known as *ki ga susumanai* (key gah sue-sue-
mah-nie), which means something like "my spirit is not
satisfied." Doi says the Japanese have been conditioned over
the centuries to feel a profound sense of dissatisfaction and
unease until they finish whatever task they are embarked
upon or they achieve whatever goal they have set for themselves. When the goal is a great one or is limitless, Doi says
there is no end to the dissatisfaction the Japanese feel, and
therefore, there is no end to their compulsion to work at a
furious pace.

This *ki ga susumanai* would also seem to help explain the
obsession the Japanese have with size and rank, as well as the
compulsion they have to be number one in everything.

Ichiban To Biri
Feeling Superior and Inferior

One of the most significant obstacles to understanding between the Japanese and outsiders—whether businessmen,
politicians, or diplomats—might be called the "two-faced"
aspect of the typical Japanese character.

The Americans, Germans, English, and French in particular have traditionally been afflicted with a very conspicuous
and destructive superiority complex that is a distinctive facet
of their national characters.

The Japanese also harbor a superiority complex that is as
strong if not stronger than that of most other nationalities.
But in the case of the Japanese, their national character is far
more complicated because they are also subject at the same
time to an intense inferiority complex.

The core of the traditional Japanese superiority complex
probably derived from the ancient mythological theme that
Japan was created by divine beings and that the Japanese
themselves, however indirectly, were descendants of these

same superior creatures. (A concept, I might add, that has long since disappeared in postfeudal generations.) In any event, this basic cultural concept of superiority gradually became stronger over the centuries because of unchallenged insular nationalism and an inbred life-style that was eventually refined to delicate perfection. Cultural historians say the idea gained further stature when the Mongols attempted to invade Japan in 1174 and again in 1180, and both times were routed by the "divine" intervention of one of the country's seasonal typhoons (giving rise to the *kami kaze* or "divine wind" idea).

Development of the feudalistic samurai warrior code from the eleventh to the fifteenth centuries added pride and a remarkable capacity for arrogance to the convictions of superiority that had been growing in the Japanese from the dawn of their history.

When the first Westerners began arriving in Japan in the fifteenth and sixteenth centuries, the Japanese became even move convinced of their superiority in all important social and cultural pursuits. To them, the Westerners looked and often behaved like half-wild savages. They were large, hairy, often dirty, and in contrast to the exquisitely well-behaved Japanese, had the manners of uncivilized barbarians.

The Japanese subsequently developed considerable admiration for the technical and material accomplishments of Westerners, but they continued to regard themselves as superior to Americans and Europeans in matters of the spirit and heart.

The inferior side of the Japanese "face" no doubt had its origin in Japan's relationships with Korea and China, beginning around the third century A.D. and lasting well beyond the eighth century. At the start of this period, Japan was divided into numerous competing clans, with primitive lifestyles, while China was at the height of one of its greatest dynasties and Korea had long been the cultural beneficiary of its huge neighbor. The impact this cultural disparity had on the Japanese mind is still very much in evidence.

The big difference between Japan's relationship with China well over a thousand years ago and with the West today is that the Japanese could at least identify with the Chinese racially and emotionally, thus lessening the trauma resulting from their inferior position.

In contrast, the typical Japanese today finds it difficult or impossible to identify with Caucasian and black Westerners. Not only does the Westerner's appearance irrevocably separate him from the Japanese, many of his attitudes and manners are diametrically opposed to "the Japanese Way" and are alien and shocking.

At the same time, most Japanese continue to envy Americans and some Europeans for their living standards, their individualism, their social and economic freedoms, and even for their size and light-colored skin. The Japanese thus feel both superior and inferior to Westerners at the same time, with considerably more passion than they regard other Orientals.

Probably the one thing in which the Japanese now take the greatest pride and which makes them feel the most superior to other people (since defeat in war shattered the belief of their spiritual superiority) is their "humanism." The Japanese have long tended to believe that their social attitudes and institutions are the most human of all, and at least until recent decades, they were imbued with a deep belief that it was their duty to spread their own brand of humanism and harmony to the rest of the world.

As the world well knows, the Japanese have now achieved technological and economic par with the leading countries of the West. This accomplishment has noticeably increased their feelings of superiority, but their feelings of inferiority remain a disrupting, emotional influence in their lives because they are now primarily related to racial characteristics that are absolute and to the miniscule size and economic vulnerability of their country.

Among other things, their sense of inferiority gives the Japanese an overwhelming desire to catch and surpass all other countries, with the result that they are accused of being "too ambitious, too hardworking." During the 1960s and 1970s, they came close to destroying both their health and environment for the sake of economic growth.

The Japanese will not be able to rid themselves of this feeling of inferiority until they learn a new set of practical and spiritual values which give them a new respect for the individual, his worth and his responsibilities. They must learn at the same time to accept differences in ideas, in people, and in customs, without constantly comparing and measuring their traditional way of life against foreign standards.

As for the future influence of the superiority complex of the Japanese, it seems to me that just as the Romans of long ago, the Germans in more recent years, and now the Americans have had to accept the fact that they are not endowed with any special ability or divine right to be masters of the world, the Japanese must also purge themselves of this ancient, egoistic impulse.

On the personal, individual level, the Japanese—like most other nationalities—must recognize and accept the idea that on the average they are no better and no worse than other people, and that neither their inferiority feelings nor their superiority feelings have any inherent, natural basis in fact.

Once rid of both of these false, misleading, and dangerous assumptions, the Japanese will find themselves much more comfortable and effective in their international relationships.

Mono-No-Aware
Aesthetics in Business

The Japanese, like most Asians, were traditionally as concerned with emotional and spiritual things as they were with material things. This attitude led to the development of a culture in which aesthetics often took precedence over reason. Natural beauty, and things made of basic materials in a "natural" way, became objects of worship. Communing with nature through poetry and various aesthetic appreciation "cults" were intimate parts of every person's life.

Takeo Doi says the Japanese preoccupation with aesthetics throughout their history was caused by their urge to *amaeru* with nature. Thus the practices involving flowers, the moon, snow, and even the sounds of insects are, in Dio's view, direct manifestations of the *amae* factor in Japanese culture. Doi reasons that the innate hunger of the Japanese for *amae* is so strong it cannot be satisfied—there is literally no way to remerge mother and child nor merge the individual adult and nature (the cosmos).

As usual, there are several key words in Japanese that pertain to the role of aesthetics and communion with nature in Japan. One is *mono-no-aware* (moe-no-no-ah-wah-ray), which refers to an extraordinary sensitivity to nature, to beauty, and the ability to merge one's identity with that of an object or mood, especially one that is tinged with recognition of the impermanence of all things.

Another, more commonly used word is *shibui* (she-buu-ee), which refers to beauty that is in perfect harmony with nature and has a tranquil effect upon the viewer.* Then there is *sabi* (sah-bee), an attribute of beauty sometimes called "the rust of the ages"—moss on a rock or tree, wrinkles on the face of an aged man or woman, waste wood bleached gray by the weather. *Wabi* (wah-bee) denotes another aspect of beauty in the Japanese lexicon. It refers to materials that are the epitome of simplicity and austerity. *Yugen* (yuu-gain), "mystery" or "subtlety," connotes a type of beauty, dear to the Japanese, that "lies modestly beneath the surface of things."

There are more such descriptive words, all providing additional insights into the extraordinary role of aestheticism in the distinctive life-style developed by the Japanese; all aimed at achieving a deep, satisfying sense of identity with nature— and now giving the Japanese a significant advantage in product design and packaging.

At the same time, beauty was not all tranquil harmony to the Japanese. There was another side of aesthetics expressed in the term *iki* (ee-key), which suggests wit, flair, stylishness, and sophistication. *Iki* beauty refers to objects as well as character, habits, and personality of the individual. The person with *iki* is cool and smooth, and floats through life with savoir faire.

The tradition of communing with nature through practices elevated to the level of aesthetic cults has considerably waned among the younger generations in Japan, but enough of it remains that some aesthetic appreciation and artistic skill is

---

*For a detailed discussion of the aesthetic practices of the Japanese, and their value to the rest of the world, see *Japanese Secrets of Graceful Living* by Boye De Mente.

considered essential to the complete individual.

On the business side, many companies offer employees free classes in aesthetic pursuits such as flower arranging, dancing, and the tea ceremony. The older and more successful the businessman, the more he tends to concern himself with spiritual and emotional contentment obtained through either artistic or aesthetic activities. He may look down on, or at least feel sorry for, the executive who is too busy or too insensitive to do likewise.

Foreign businessmen who are serious about getting to know and establishing a lasting rapport with their Japanese counterparts are well advised to also cultivate an appreciation for simple beauty and the myriad workings of nature.

Kanjo Wo Sasuru
Emotional Strokes

Japanese who have not been Westernized—which means the majority—are generally ill at ease in the company of Westerners, even if they speak enough of a foreign language to communicate on a basic level. They simply have not been conditioned to engage in casual freewheeling conversations with anyone except longtime Japanese friends.

Americans are often the most difficult for the Japanese to associate with. Our loose, back-slapping manner is exactly the type of behavior they were traditionally trained to avoid. As mentioned earlier, the penalty for breaching social etiquette in Feudal Japan was extremely serious, and in some cases carried the death sentence, a circumstance that helped make "proper" behavior second nature to the Japanese.

The Japanese, as of course do other societies, have a prescribed form and manner for every familiar situation that might arise. When a situation does come up that is outside their normal experience and over which they have no control, they are at a loss for what to do and undergo intense discomfort and embarrassment.

Most Japanese, as much as they might like to, cannot become close to a foreigner and cannot enjoy a mutually satisfying relationship which transcends their differences—except

124 JAPANESE ETIQUETTE AND ETHICS IN BUSINESS

on a purely physical basis. This also holds true in reverse. It is
the rare foreigner who can overcome his own attitudes, values, rules, and other social instincts and replace them with a
new set that requires him to either be bicultural or blot out his
own personality.

The Japanese are programmed, by a deep desire to make a
favorable impression, to give every indication that they
wholeheartedly enjoy intercourse with foreigners. At the
same time, they are also conditioned to abhor contact with
outsiders and to look upon them as dangerous competitors, if
not outright enemies. This provides for a strange paradox.
They crave to be liked and admired, but from a distance.
They are repelled by the thought of intimacy with a foreigner
and yet force themselves to go through the motions.

Thus for the Westerner to function smoothly in a Japanese
business setting requires an extraordinary amount of subtlety, even a sixth sense, to maintain the delicate balance between ambiguity and the concrete, the suggestive and the
direct and decisive. Probably the biggest danger in any such
setting is the tendency of the foreigner to say too much,
compounding the possibility for error or friction. In fact, one
of the biggest mistakes many American businessmen make in
their dealings with the Japanese is talking too much, overstat-
ing their case. There is a tendency for the Japanese to assume
that anyone who talks a lot and repeats himself in an effort to
make a point or to persuade is insincere and possibly trying to
pull a fast one.

The Japanese business system works less on cold objectivity
and logic and more on emotion. In virtually all confronta-
tions, the appeal that usually wins in the end is the emotional
one—for harmony, for face, for the future benefit of the
majority, etc. Emotion is the glue that binds the Japanese
system together. If you want to get along with, influence, or
lead a Japanese employee, associate, or client, see to his emotional needs first.

Not surprisingly, the Japanese regard most Americans as
rikutsu-poi (ree-kute-sue-poy)—too logical, too objective, too
uncaring about the emotional (human) content in business
relations.

Western businessmen should keep in mind that the first

and often primary reaction of most Japanese to any subject is generally emotional, then ethnic and then nationalistic; and it is essential that any approach to them be tailored to bypass or get through this conditioned response. This is particularly important when the topic at hand has political implications, because the Japanese responses to these topics adversely affect U.S.-Japan relations—businessmen who know better keep their honest thoughts to themselves.

Foreign politicians who go to Tokyo and make what they feel are rational, reasonable, and practical dissertations on Japan's "invisible" trade barriers, pointing out example after example, are often stopped cold when a ranking Japanese journalist gets up and says something like, "Senator, what we really want to hear is what you think about the Japanese people."

Put on the spot, the stunned senator has no choice but to say he admires the Japanese and thinks they are a superior people. The journalists then go on to write that foreign businessmen have trouble getting into the Japanese market because they are not willing to do things the Japanese way, not because of any barriers blocking their entry.

The Japanese maintain that the problem is one of perception. They say the market "appears closed" because foreigners do not understand the Japanese way of doing business and do not make sufficient effort to learn. Thus when Japanese and foreign politicians meet to discuss economic problems, they are generally on different wavelengths and talk about different things.

One of the ways to get around the Japanese tendency to view everything on an ethnic and emotional basis is to acknowledge the emotional, personal factors at the outset, giving them sufficient due so that the Japanese can relate to you as an understanding and caring human being, and then get down to logical, practical concerns.

Moretsu Shain
The "Gung-Ho" Employees

Although Japan had emerged as one of the top manufacturing nations of the world by 1960, it was not until the 1970s that the Japanese really hit their stride as salesmen. This has to be explained and qualified.

Selling, especially in the positive, aggressive manner practiced by Americans and some Europeans, is diametrically opposed to several of the primary themes of traditional Japanese culture. In traditional Japanese behavior, a forward, aggressive approach was forbidden. The Japanese were taught, quite literally forced, to be reticent, self-effacing, to speak in vague terms, to avoid bragging, to deprecate themselves and their belongings, and to be repelled by the opposite kind of behavior.

During the many centuries before Japan began doing business with the West, about the only type of aggressive selling one saw was by barkers touting goods at retail shops and at stands during festive occasions. Then, following industrialization, new methods of doing business did not develop which would have resulted in the widespread use of salesmen. Japan became a nation of neighborhood shopkeepers, tiny factories, and a few dozen *zaibatsu* monopolistic combines.

It was not until about 1950 that Japanese companies began paying attention to their sales departments. As late as the mid-1950s, it was the worst kind of insult to suggest to a college graduate that he become a salesman. It was equivalent to seriously proposing that a Yale or Harvard man get himself a shoeshine box and go to work on the sidewalks.

During the 1950s and early 1960s, salesmanship in Japan also suffered because the average young employee placed in the sales or export department of his company had no "feel" for the merchandise he was supposed to sell. Not knowing his products intimately and, in many cases, being unfamiliar with the way they were used, the manufacturer-exporter was at considerable disadvantage when he attempted to sell to Westerners on any basis other than price. He was also handicapped by not knowing the psychology of the people he wanted to sell to and by not wanting to make a mistake or be laughed at.

During the 1960s, several major Japanese companies ran elaborate television commercials designed to change the popular image of aggressive selling and sales people from negative to positive. At the same time, the young people coming of age during this period had not been conditioned to dislike or avoid aggressive behavior. Other consumer attitudes and habits were also changing during these years. By the mid-1970s, the Japanese style of "passive selling" had more or less been relegated to urban pockets of traditionalism and to distant rural areas.

The popular image of the "new" Japanese that emerged in the late 1960s and early 1970s was often described by the term *moretsu shain* (moe-ray-t'sue shah-een), or the "gung-ho" employee who works at top speed and seemingly never relaxes. The connotation becomes clearer when you consider that *moretsu* literally means "fury" or "violence."

In international business, the Japanese are now sometimes criticized for overselling, and for not being sensitive to the feelings of some of their potential customers, particularly in Southeast Asian countries. Now instead of being handicapped by poor salesmanship, or no salesmanship at all, the Japanese are handicapped by a general inability to deal effectively with cross-cultural relationships. They are acutely aware of the problem, however, and are carrying out educational and cross-cultural sensitization programs to help overcome it.

8

Matome
Summing Up

Humanism Plus Authoritarianism

Generally speaking, Japan's management philosophy is based on a subtle balance of "humanism mixed with authoritarianism" and is patterned after the Japanese adaptation of an ideal Confucian family. In Confucian ethics, the ideal family is one that follows the Five Principles: filial piety, fidelity, obedience, kindness, and loyalty to one's superior.

When the Japanese imported Confucianism from China, they switched the order of the Five Principles, making loyalty to one's superior paramount, so the principles would fit more readily with their own already existing authoritarian system.

Thereafter, the repression of one's own opinions and feelings, along with automatic submission to superior authority, was made second nature to the Japanese by the systematic application of intense physical and psychological pressures, backed up by swift punishment for anyone who resisted.

The authoritarian nature of this feudal family system of enterprise management was greatly tempered, however, by the broad application of a philosophy of humanism which had also been a traditional characteristic of the Japanese since ancient times. This humanism was a fundamental belief, Shinto in origin, that people should be selfless and kind and help each other, that one who is in a superior position is morally obligated to take care of those who work for or serve

him, and that peaceful harmony should be maintained by
strict adherence to these beliefs.

The Parent-Child Ethic

Japan's distinctive humanism-plus-authoritarianism business
system was translated into action in the form of a parent-child
relationship. The employer was looked upon as a combination mother and father, and the employees were his "children." Interpersonal relations between the two ideally followed the rearranged Confucian principles, just as they were
applied to private family life in Feudal Japan.

The particular strength of the typical large-scale Japanese
company today springs from the traditional social manners
and ethics as these were developed in the folds of the old
feudal family system. For centuries, people were taught to
respect authority and to work cooperatively. In return for
this, they were guaranteed a livelihood and protection. The
system was held together and made to function by minutely
defined personal obligations and a highly refined etiquette
system. The focal points of the various controlling obligations
were the central government (the Shogunate), the clan, the
family, and finally the individual.

The introduction of individualism and democracy into Japan in 1868 weakened and in some cases completely severed
these feudalistic, obligatory ties. With the changeover to an
industrial economy in the 1880s and 1890s, the means of
earning a living became the focal point in the lives of the
Japanese. Company affiliation automatically replaced the
clan, and to some extent the family as well, in the social fabric
of the country. Businessmen inherited the loyalty, the respect, and the service once given to the clan and the feudal
government.

The development of modern industry in Japan thus was a
primary factor in the breaking up of the feudal patterns in
home life, but at the same time, the larger enterprises, especially, continued the functions of the old family and clan
units, each company being a great family of its own in which
the traditional patterns of obligation, loyalty, and conduct
have continued in only slightly diminished force.

The Western business executive who approaches a large Japanese company should therefore keep in mind that he is dealing with a "family" in which the members are ranked vertically according to their seniority and position, and that with only rare exceptions one member cannot commit the "family" to anything. The Japanese executive on whatever level must obtain the advice and consent of his "company relatives."

It must be recognized that the relationship between the larger Japanese employer and his employees is not strictly an economic one. The average employer gets from his workers a degree of loyalty, cooperation, and effort that is seldom surpassed anywhere. In turn, the employer not only feels responsible for the economic welfare of his employees but also takes an interest in their social and spiritual well-being.

This feeling of mutual obligation is repeated on every level in Japanese company management, with each responsible person doing his best to take care of those under him. The higher a person rises in management, the stronger this feeling tends to become. The more successful a Japanese businessman, the more generous he tends to become and the more he tries to do for his "family."

The distinctive Japanese family-company system is changing fairly rapidly under pressure from uncontrollable economic factors, but enough of it still remains to give Japanese companies and Japanese company management a special character of their own.

"Marine Corps" Management

One of the best ways to gain a quick "surface" insight into Japanese management philosophy and practices is to relate each company or organization to a military unit, particularly to the United States Marine Corps, operating under the "old book" of strict discipline in which rank and seniority are the foundation of all relationships.

Under this system every "enlistment" in a major Japanese corporation is, in principle, for the working life of the individual. Those with grade school and high school educations start as privates and eventually may become noncommissioned officers (blue-collar workers, supervisors, and foremen). All university graduates automatically become officer candidates (management trainees) when they "enlist," and all expect to be promoted to successively higher officer ranks as they build up longevity.

Pay scales are primarily based on longevity in service and rank, with promotions determined by time-in-grade, schooling, and other qualifications. The company lapel button is the "uniform" and the title on the name-card denotes rank. The *ojigi*, or bow, is the equivalent of the military salute. Inferiors are expected to pay proper respect to superiors and to obey them without question. Superiors are responsible for both the good and bad actions of their subordinates and can win and keep their respect and support only by taking care of them.

Just as the outsider generally does not enter the Marine Corps as a sergeant or captain, the Japanese company requires, with still only a few exceptions, that its noncommissioned officers (blue-collar foremen) and officers (managers) come up through the ranks—and thus have a proper understanding and appreciation of the required manners and ethics.

Just as the different branches of the armed forces tend to compete with each other for everything from funds to research projects, so do Japanese companies. Within Japanese companies there is also the same sectional and departmental rivalry that was traditionally promoted in every military organization, from squads of foot-soldiers up to armies.

Activities within sections and departments in Japanese companies are very much like those in a squad, platoon, or company of Marines, with similar attitudes toward responsibility and loyalty to their branch of service.

Just as military personnel are generally promoted to higher ranks according to their educational background (high school, university, academy, etc.), they also concern themselves with dates of promotion so that within the rank of captain, for example, Captain Smith outranks Captain Jones because Smith was promoted first and therefore has more time-in-grade.

Just as a well-trained and highly motivated squad of marines can naturally be expected to do well in battle, a Japanese group does particularly well in situations demanding close, cooperative teamwork. As in the military, the independent spirit or the innovator fares well in Japan only if he or she is capable of working within the group, forgoing personal ambitions and recognition.

Again, a primary advantage of the Japanese system of vertically ranking each individual and each group, and the various rules that govern the system, is that it can be galvanized for almost instant action and can automatically be expected to perform like a well-drilled infantry squad. Each team member is responsible not only for his own but also his teammate's livelihood, and regardless of how he personally feels about the people he works with or what he is charged with doing, he is under extraordinary pressure to do his best.

The Emotional/Sensual Element

Despite the cultural idiosyncrasies that make Japanese and Western businessmen so different in attitudes, manners, and methods, most Westerners who have been to Japan—and especially the men—are very strongly attracted to life among the Japanese.

This attraction is emotional and may be separated into two categories, the intellectual and the sexual. Both of these areas are important, but the influence of the latter is often the strongest and certainly the most obvious.

There are two sides—and several facets—to the intellectual/emotional category. One side is the very strong sense of superiority that Westerners still feel toward the Japanese. Because of racial and cultural prejudices, average Westerners, living or traveling in Japan, are able to delude themselves into believing they are better than even the most accomplished, wealthy, or famous Japanese, regardless of their character or learning.

The other side of the intellectual category, which attracts all foreigners in varying degrees, including the most stupid ones, is that which appeals both consciously and subconsciously to their aesthetic sense and to their admiration—from a distance—of some of the more benign aspects of Japan's unique civilization. Things Japanese that, in their own contexts, are pleasing to foreigners include traditional wearing apparel, handicrafts, architecture, landscape gardening, and the rigid formality of Japanese etiquette.

There is also a very strong sense of the exotic surrounding everything that has survived from Old Japan, and this added dash of the romantic and mysterious contributes to the aesthetic pleasure experienced by foreigners confronted with a traditional Japanese scene.

The sexual category pertains almost entirely to men, and it applies especially to those who were steeped in the Puritan-Christian concept that sex is basically sinful and that monogamy and/or abstinence are moral virtues.

In Japan, sex has never had the stigma of evil. On the contrary, it has always been considered an important part of living, playing a vital role in the native religion of the country, as well as having been sanctioned as a pleasure. There were traditionally different sexual moralities for men and women in Japan, however. Generally, all men considered that they had a right to unconcealed sexual promiscuity, the volume and variety depending only on what each individual could afford. Women, on the other hand, were divided into two groups: those known as "public women" who worked away from their homes in inns, tea houses, restaurants, drinking establishments, red-light districts, etc.; and women who did not work outside their homes—the famous *o'josan* (oh-joe-sahn), who were brought up under very strict conditions and were usually, of course, the daughters of the better-to-do.

The *o'josan* and the wives of the privileged samurai warrior class, and in particular the nobility, were not ascetics, however. Throughout most of Japan's history, they engaged in love affairs whenever possible, and they were not subject to pangs of moral guilt or criticism stemming from a belief that virginity or marital faithfulness was a divine virtue. About the only difference between the public and "private" women of Japan, as far as their attitude toward sexual morality was concerned, was time, place, and partner.

In Old Japan, lower class women, who were the majority, as well as women of rank, were pretty much at the mercy of the proud, haughty samurai who carried their male prerogative as far as their audacity and means would allow. The great chain of over 75,000 travelers' inns that flourished during the long Tokugawa era (1603-1868) functioned as nightly "love-tels." Legal and illegal red-light districts also flourished until April Fool's Day in 1956 (with a one-year grace period to go out of business).

Today in Japan, the situation is pretty much the same as far as volume and variety of sexual activities are concerned. There are no concentrated, marked pleasure quarters, but there are more "public" girls, and the pampered daughter of the well-to-do is more apt to be abroad at night than the less fortunate girl who works in some office or store.

Since Japanese tend to be as sexually active as their financial position allows and their inclinations dictate, it takes a large number of female partners to keep up with the demand. Most of these are provided by the famous *mizu shobai*, literally "water business," or entertainment trades, which were discussed in Chapter 5.

In addition to the one-time liaisons between customers of these business establishments and their female employees, there is also widespread sexual activity among couples in the business and social world who become acquainted and then date. This includes older married men, who are usually in a much better position to carry on an outside affair because of their higher income brackets.

Most of the non-*mizu shobai* women concerned are single, but it is not unusual for married women to have occasional or full-time lovers—especially since a significant percentage of their husbands not only carry on extramarital affairs but also often spend nights away from home on company business.

There are dozens of thousands of inns and hundreds of hotels throughout Japan that exist by renting rooms—with bath if desired—to couples who use them for only an hour or so. Tokyo's Roppongi district is especially well known for such hotels, but there are dozens of them throughout the huge city. Most of the famous resort areas, such as Atami and Ito, depend to a considerable extent upon the weekend patronage of trysting couples to keep them flourishing. These very common weekend trips are often referred to—by the men, at least—as "weekend honeymoons," and the men who go on them regularly, with different girls as often as possible, refer to their partners as "weekend brides." I have known a number of men who boasted they had had a different "weekend bride" almost every weekend for a period of several years.

Not having a sense of guilt about indulging in sex, the Japanese look at it in an entirely different light than what has been traditional among "Christianized" Westerners. At the same time, the idea that a girl who is not a virgin has endangered her chances of making a good marriage has been present in Japan since ancient times. It seems, however, that this belief is not nearly strong enough to counterbalance the other attitudes toward sex—one of which, in several parts of Japan, has included "trial marriages" by couples who were attracted to each other. The boy and girl lived together, usually in the girl's home, for a few weeks or months to find out if they could get along. If they couldn't, and the girl wasn't pregnant, the boy returned home and started looking elsewhere.

It should not be surprising, therefore, that when the average Westerner finds himself in a society that still condones—in practice, if no longer in principle—sexual promiscuity, he is apt to take to it like a duck to water. Some, in fact, go overboard. They are not content with a more or less full-time mistress or the occasional "short-time." They work at it systematically and take great pride in their "conquests."

In addition to the attraction provided by actual sexual contact, there is a sensuality and sexuality pervading Japanese culture that gives off a constant promise of sex. This promise is a powerful stimulant to the average Westerner, and it is the *appeal* of this distinctive atmosphere that holds many outsiders to Japan, rather than actual pleasures of the flesh.

Of course, much of the appeal of this sexual promise is provided by the Westerner's imagination. But there are in truth a number of qualities or characteristics possessed by most Japanese women—besides their general availability—that (when in a Japanese setting) give them definite advantages over Western women and often make this promise a reality. These include many of the qualities traditionally considered ideal in women by sexist-minded men.

Lafcadio Hearn, the original Japanophile—who later, after he had had time to really see behind the "Japanese mask," severely criticized Japan's social system—said that foreigners were attracted to (turn-of-the-century) Japan because it was like living in an illusion of some future paradise. He said this illusion of paradise was provided by the etiquette cult of the Japanese, which on the surface presented a picture of perfect harmony. There were also the old ideals of Shintoism, which included instinctive unselfishness, a universal sense of moral beauty, and a common desire to find joy in life by making happiness for others.

The Kindness Syndrome

For every example of a "bad" or "obnoxious" habit or manner that the Japanese have (from the Western viewpoint), a good or pleasing characteristic can also be pointed to, and it is obvious that the good side outweighs the bad. In many years of living and working in Japan, I have had so many special kindnesses extended to me that at times it has been embarrassing. Foreign visitors to Japan invariably have a number of such experiences with the Japanese that are genuine—and sometimes startling—demonstrations of unselfish kindness.

My younger sister Rebecca, who visited Tokyo as a tourist, went off on her own one day to find the office of a steamship company. Since the addressing system in Japan has nothing to do with the street on which a building is located (and most of the streets are unnamed), she became confused and ended up in the wrong section of downtown. Noticing her standing on a street corner looking perplexed, a man who couldn't speak English began trying to help her. When she was finally able to get the name of the steamship company across to him, he flagged a taxi and not only took her there but also paid the fare.

Another typical example: a friend forgot a pair of contact lenses in a taxi. Realizing they were missing as soon as the taxi pulled away, she tried to catch the driver's attention. He didn't see her frantic waving, but a young, college-student passerby did and immediately went to her aid. When he understood that she had left something in the cab, he escorted her to a police box down the street. There was no policeman on duty at the stand, so the good Samaritan stopped another passerby and explained the situation to him. The second passerby hailed a cab and took my friend to the district police station—altogether spending nearly an hour to help an utter stranger he couldn't converse with.

Such incidents, as the above imply, are common, and although the longtime foreign resident in Japan often takes them for granted, the newcomer is immensely impressed and enthusiastic in his praise for the Japanese.

This very strong human element, which is characteristic of the Japanese when they are in their own environment and at peace with themselves and others, helps making living and working in Japan tolerable and often more satisfying than living back home.

Sources of Japan's Strength

In addition to the human element that cancels out many of the attitudes and habits of the Japanese that are negative and disadvantageous, there are other factors, psychological and sociological, that explain why the Japanese, despite their failings, are a formidable race and why Japan is one of the world's top industrial powers.

The first and most important of these factors has been the willingness of the Japanese to sacrifice. From earliest times the Japanese were taught and conditioned to believe that it was a virtue to devote their labor and their lives to fulfill the various obligations that were the essence of their society.

This willingness to sacrifice has been the one prevailing ethic by which the people lived through the centuries and which made possible the development of all the various attitudes and habits that distinguish the Japanese from other people. Until the coming of economic affluence in the 1960s, it was visible in every aspect of their society.

Along with this willingness to sacrifice came a willingness to be regimented and homogenized. The Japanese became alike mentally and socially to such an extent that they more or less functioned as a single unit, as one giant family with a common head. The secret of the nation's rise to the heady heights of a world power is simply that most everybody worked together for the same end for considerably less personal benefit than workers in other industrialized countries.

Another factor that also tempers to a great extent the more harsh aspects of Japanese society and at the same time contributes to the industrial prowess of Japan is the very deep and broad stream of aestheticism permeating the traditional culture. This stream of aestheticism was so deeply intertwined within the traditional life-style of the Japanese that it was part of their cultural inheritance, something they learned and applied as part of being Japanese. Until as late as the 1950s, the Japanese seemed to inherit not solely a sense of but a desire for harmony in all things—in their selection of colors, architecture, handicrafts, apparel, dimensions, speech, and actions, including such violent ones as suicide.

Factors that played leading roles in the development of an aesthetic civilization in Japan include the powerful influence of Shinto and Zen Buddhism, the capsule size of the country, the remarkable homogeneity of the people, the all-powerful Confucian-oriented feudal government under which the Japanese lived for so many centuries, and long before this, some distinctive trait in the people that seems always to have been present.

One of the most interesting of these influences was Zen Buddhism, as manifested in the tea ceremony, which is still widely practiced in Japan. To those with only a cursory knowledge of Japan and the Japanese, describing the familiar, but little understood, tea ceremony as anything more than "tea with some rules" may sound farfetched, but to declare that the tea ceremony is one of the principal manifestations for much that is called "Japanese" may sound strange indeed. Nevertheless, it is so.

As practiced by the Japanese, the tea ceremony is essentially a worship of the natural and an attempt to achieve perfect harmony with nature and the cosmos. The tea room, the most important accessory in the tea ceremony, is a different world; it is free from all vulgarity, free from the slightest distraction, so that one can surrender oneself completely to the adoration of natural beauty, to striving for physical and spiritual union.

It is unfortunate that this ceremony has not been better explained by the Japanese or better understood in the West, for what most foreigners regard as a simple demonstration of a Japanese custom (the results of which are a bitter and to the uninitiated "distasteful" tea) is in reality the only instance in which the unselfish appreciation of simple, natural beauty has become a national cult.

As a result of the remarkable aesthetic sense of the Japanese, there is a subtle charm and in many cases an exquisite beauty in the basic form and decorative design of native Japanese products. It is this distinctive charm and beauty, called *shibui* in Japanese, that captured the imagination of the Western world when Japan first became known to the West.

The aesthetic theme is still conspicuous in Japan today, although there is a tremendous gap between the attitudes and practices of older people and the younger generation. The theme is obviously weakening under the onslaught of Western products and ideas, but it is still there in the language, architecture, arts, crafts, and the remnants of the traditional life-style. It still provides the Japanese of all ages with an unique source of strength and satisfaction that is sorely lacking in other industrial societies.

Pride, Prejudice, and Perseverance

The Japanese have always been a fantastically proud people, and when they have the opportunity, they are just as ambitious. This pride and burning ambition to prove their superiority, or at least their equality, accounts for a great deal of their strength, energy, and perseverance. They are constantly measuring their accomplishments against the world's best or the world's largest. The more successful they are, the more convinced they become that their way is the right way.

The fact that Japan has been amazingly successful in recent decades has convinced most older Japanese businessmen that their business system, which is an outgrowth of their national character, is the best in the world. Japanese businessmen are envious of some of the freewheeling options enjoyed be Western businessmen, in particular Americans, but they are also critical of the American system because to them it is "inhuman" and debasing. They are quick to point out that American management techniques to not "fit" the character and preference of the Japanese.

The Japanese are, in fact, virtually obsessed with their national character, and they spend a great deal of time and money studying it. These studies show that the Japanese generally consider themselves happy and contented, and that they regard themselves as the hardest working, the most diligent, politest, kindest, and most patient people in the world. The typical Japanese businessman is always very much concerned about upholding the honor of Japan and the Japanese in dealings with outsiders. In his own mind, he never acts alone. He is acting for and under the scrutiny of all Japanese.

It is still typical of Japanese businessmen to assume a humble stance in the presence of visitors. This often gives the resident or visiting Western businessman a high feeling of superiority—and frequently leads him to underestimate the Japanese and to commit excesses. The Japanese businessman is simply being polite and treating the foreigner as an honored guest.

Virtually all management personnel in larger Japanese companies are university graduates and regard themselves as an elite group and as intellectuals. It is also characteristic of those who have gone into the government ministries to harbor a certain amount of cultural, racial, and political prejudice against the world at large and to regard themselves as Japan's first bulwark of defense against "excessive" foreign business encroachment. They are not averse, however, to learning all they can from outsiders and adapting the knowledge to their own advantage.

The Japanese executive is deeply committed to the management system in his own company because, in the ways that count, his company is his life. The penalty for not conforming, for breaking the traditional pattern, is very serious. If he should step out of line, he is either shunted aside or ostracized—and unless he has very powerful connections, he has practically no chance of being taken in by another company of comparable standing.

Individually, the Japanese businessman is not bound by immutable principles of good, bad, or logic in the American sense. He adapts easily and readily to suit the circumstances and has a starkly realistic attitude toward power and what suits his (and Japan's) best interest. The old characteristics of abhorring selfishness and regarding profit-making as a social evil have long since been relegated to the background. His life is so closely tied in with the company and the company system that his own opinions seldom count for anything.

The Japanese businessman is usually a far more complex individual than his Western counterpart and, in a different way, is subjected to a great deal more stress. Once he enters a large company as a young man, he has very little direct control over his future. He must adhere to severely demanding etiquette and ethical codes in order to avoid upsetting the harmony of the system, knowing all the while that he will most likely spend his entire working life intimately linked to the same co-workers.

The Japanese management system is geared primarily to obtain maximum cooperation from employees with a minimum of friction, and only secondarily to obtain business results. The fact that the system works extremely well is obvious.

Most Japanese executives support the system because they are so caught up in its web they must perpetuate it to survive. It is changing, however, though slowly and often imperceptibly, even in the old-line companies. These changes will accelerate as time goes on.

The Japanese are very much aware that many of their habits, customs, and attitudes seriously handicap them in their international relations. In the early 1970s, some leaders in business, government, and education began saying that the Japanese would have to become *un-Japanese* if they were really to succeed over the long haul in the outside world.

This is remarkable to contemplate because they are talking about the very fabric of their culture: their language, their values, their attitudes and manners. The Japanese are, of course, changing and becoming less "Japanese," but very slowly. Too slowly in the eyes of a growing number. In their view, among the several challenges now facing the Japanese is whether or not they can, in fact, change their national character fast enough and far enough to succeed in their goals.

Appendix
Glossary of Useful Terms

Ago (ah-go)—In Japan one leads by the *ago* (chin) instead of the nose, and instead of "turning up your nose," you "turn up your chin." The *ago* is used in various business contexts, such as when a superior disregards the feelings of subordinates and "drives them by the chin." By the same token, when an employee does his best but fails in a task, he *ago wo dashimasu* (sticks his chin out).

Aisatsu (aye-sot-sue)—Usually translated into English as "greeting," *aisatsu* has a great deal more significance in its Japanese context than "greeting" implies. The Japanese attach considerable importance to meeting their business and professional contacts in a formal, ritualized manner, on a regular basis. Some *aisatsu* meetings are routine but important, such as to introduce a new company member or new product or to express thanks for something special. The more important the occasion, the higher ranking the participants in the *aisatsu*. Prior to a major tie-up between companies, it is customary for the two presidents to hold a relatively short get-acquainted *aisatsu*. Specific details of the association are not discussed. The prime function of the high-level *aisatsu* is to put the official seal of approval on the proposed new relationship so that subordinate executives can thereafter work out the relationship in confidence. In some cases, the presidential *aisatsu* are not held until after the agreement has been worked out.

142

Aisatsu-mawari (aye-sot-sue-mah-wah-ree)—This literally means "to go around and greet or pay respects" to customers, clients, business contacts, and fellow workers, and it is an institutionalized custom after week-long New Year's holidays, as well as after an individual returns to the home office from an overseas assignment. Such courtesy calls are an integral part of Japan's business etiquette and should be adopted by foreign businessmen involved with the Japanese. It is also essential for foreign businessmen to keep in mind that very little if any business is accomplished in or with Japanese companies during this period (usually a two- or three-day period, beginning on January 4 or 5).

Aiso (aye-so)—The Japanese are noted for smiling a lot and for being exceptionally courteous and kind. Some of this behavior is, of course, sincere. Some of it, however, is professional and is called *aiso*, which is represented by the clerk, tradesman, or businessman who puts on a smiling face when greeting and dealing with customers or potential clients. Foreign businessmen should keep in mind that *aiso* is an art that the Japanese practice with considerable skill. They will often continue smiling when disappointed, shocked, or angry, which can be very misleading to someone not familiar with the Japanese way.

Aka chochin (ah-kah choe-cheen)—Literally, "red lantern," an *aka chochin* is a large globe-shaped lantern made of heavy paper pasted over a bamboo frame that is hung in the front of bars and other drinking places. It has become synonymous with nighttime entertainment. The red lights add an exotic touch to the nighttime scene in Japan's thousands of entertainment and bar districts. See also, *chotto ippai* and *hashigo-zake*.

Antei (ahn-tay-ee)—*Antei* is the sense of security/care Japanese workers expect to get from their employers. It includes explicit interest in their personal welfare outside the company and involvement in such matters as marriage and death.

Aota-gai (ah-oh-tah-guy)—Major Japanese companies hire new entry-level employees only once a year, directly from high schools and universities. High school graduates are employed as blue-collar workers. University graduates are automatically slated for office jobs.

In the days when there was a labor shortage, it became common for larger companies to begin recruiting college students a year or more before they were scheduled to graduate. This practice came to be known as *aota gai,* or "harvesting green plants."

Small and medium-sized enterprises in Japan complained bitterly about this practice and sought government help in establishing some order in the hiring process. Through government mediation, leading corporations in the country agreed to not invite job-seeking college seniors to visit them before October 1 and to not hold employment examinations before November 1.

From fifty to sixty violations of the agreement are reported to the Labor Ministry each year, but it is estimated that this reflects only a small percentage of the actual number of *aota-gai* cases annually. As observers note, as long as college seniors want to work for prestigious firms and those firms prefer to have first pick of each senior class, "green harvesting" will continue.

Asameshi-mae (ah-sah-may-she-my)—Literally "before breakfast," this term is used to indicate that something that is to be done is so simple it can be done "before breakfast"—i.e., "as easy as pie." The term is used by people boasting of their ability, as well as by people who want to flatter someone into doing something extra (by telling them it will be *asameshi-mae* for them).

Ate-uma (ah-tay-uu-mah)—In its original usage, *ate-uma* referred to a stallion brought near a mare to excite her and make her ready for the studhorse that actually was to mate with her. Nowadays it is used in reference to any device, tool, draft plan, or technique that is used to find out the true intentions of another company or party (with whom you want or plan to do business). If you are trying to sell a product or project to a certain company and mention that some other company is also interested in the deal, you are using the other company as an *ate-uma.*

Bansei-sho (bahn-say-show)—A "document of reflection," the *bansei-sho* is an official apology that the Japanese (or foreigners in Japan) are expected to write when they run afoul of the law. Individuals who express regret at having broken the law by writing a *bansei-sho* are generally given the benefit of the doubt and shown leniency—often being let off with a warning.

Banzai (bahn-zie)—Westerners are likely to associate this shout (which literally means "Ten thousand years!") with pre-World War II Japan and emperor worship (when it meant "Long live the Emperor!"), but it is now simply a joyous shout of congratulations and goodwill, meaning "Bon voyage!" "Hip, Hip, Hurrah!" and so on. It is used when seeing newly wedded couples off on their honeymoon and businessmen off on overseas assignments, or when celebrating winning a sports event, etc.

Base-up (bay-sue ah-puu)—This is an expression used (mostly) by unions in reference to their annual spring drives to win increases in the base wages of workers. (See also *Shunto*.)

Besso (base-soh)—A villa, usually in the mountains or on the seacoast, originally for recreational or retirement purposes of the well-to-do. Now, many *besso* in Japan are owned by companies and used by employees as a fringe benefit.

Boryoku ba (boe-rio-kuu bah)—This literally means a "violence bar" and refers to bars controlled by the underworld that charge unwary customers outrageous prices for their drinks (often several hundred dollars for a few drinks) and use force, if necessary, to collect from their victims. Out-of-town Japanese often become victims of this system because they almost never ask the price of anything before they buy it (because of a combination of misplaced pride and reluctance to appear "cheap"). Foreign visitors to Japan also sometimes wander into these places and order without inquiring about the price. If the price is not posted or on a menu, ask. If it is too much, walk out.

Bottoru-kipu (bote-toe-rue-keep-puu)—It is common practice for Japanese businessmen to buy bottles of Scotch (usually) at favorite bars and have them kept there ("bottle-keep"). When they patronize these bars, they pay only for set-ups (which can be more expensive than a drink in typical bars outside Japan). The system is popular because it is another way of becoming a member of a group and having "face" in the entertainment world. Businessmen frequently take foreign guests to their *bottoru-kipu* bars.

Bucho dairi (buu-choe die-ree)—*Dairi* means "agent," "deputy," or "assistant." A *bucho dairi* is therefore an assistant department head. A *kacho dairi* is a deputy section chief.

Bureiko (buu-ray-koe)—Social and business etiquette in Japan is such that during the normal course of activity, there are very strict rules of behavior that prevent people from being informal and casual. This deeply ingrained social system prevents people from "being themselves" and from developing close, personal relationships during working hours. To counter this, the system provides brief periods when the rules of etiquette may be ignored or broken. This is known as going *bureiko*, or without etiquette, and applies to such events as year-end and New Year's parties, athletic field meets, and nighttime drinking sessions. *Bureiko* is made up of three compounds or words that mean "absence," "respect," and "form." *Burei* is usually translated as "impoliteness" or "rudeness." *Bureiko* can be translated as an "informal party."

Chochin kiji (choe-cheen kee-jee)—A *chochin* is a paper lantern and a *kiji* is a newspaper article. A *chochin kiji* is an article that "sheds light" on some company product or topic, and refers to news articles that are favorable to a company or individual. Such articles often accompany advertisements, sometimes appearing on the same page or at least in the same section of the publication as the ad. The Japanese version of a "puff article."

Chorei Shiki (choe-ray she-kee)—The *Chorei Shiki*, "Morning Greeting Ceremony," is a traditional custom in the offices (departments) of most larger Japanese companies. The employees stand, face the manager, and all bow to one another and call out morning greetings. The manager then ordinarily makes announcements or comments on whatever is appropriate. In some companies, these morning sessions include rousing pep talks and end with the singing of company songs. The ceremonies are an important part of the group orientation and communal spirit of Japanese management.

Chotto ippai (chote-toe eep-pie)—This is a colloquial phrase that has come to mean "Let's have a quick drink." It is another institutionalized practice that plays a key role in interpersonal relations of company employees. Since frank and personal conversations are almost never held in the office during working hours, the custom is to have a drink, or two or three, after hours and talk about concerns or problems in an informal atmosphere. A great deal of Japan's business communication takes place during *chotto ippai* sessions at bars.

Chotto muzukashi (chote-toe muu-zuu-kah-she)—When a Japanese businessman, politician, or anyone else says, "*chotto muzukashi*" ("It's a little difficult"), it is usually a polite way of saying no or "it can't be done" or "I can't do it." Not understanding the true meaning of the term, the foreign businessman is likely to continue trying aggressively to get the Japanese businessman to accept or agree to whatever he wants, even though it is a little difficult. The foreigner's presentation often includes how it can be done "easily."

Chuto saiyo (chuu-toe sie-yoe)—Larger Japanese companies normally hire only once a year, in the spring, directly from schools (see also *teiki-saiyo*). When they do hire at other times during the year, and this is usually only in the case of a special need or emergency (such as a sudden expansion or the need for someone highly skilled in a special area), it is known as *chuto saiyo* or "midstream hiring." Employees hired during "midstream" by larger firms, especially if they have worked for other companies, may be regarded as something less than "pure" company people for the rest of their working careers.

Daikoku bashira (die-koe-kuu bah-she-rah)—The literal meaning of *daikoku bashira* is something like "good fortune divinity pillar," which came to mean the main pillar in a building or house that holds up the entire structure. It is now often used in reference to an especially capable or productive individual or product on which a company or organization depends. Despite the diffusion of responsibility and achievement in the typical Japanese group, there is often a single, outstanding individual who is recognized as the group's *daikoku bashira* and to whom the group will defer. A product that is responsible for a significant percentage of company sales is also referred to as a *daikoku bashira*. (See also *Yataibone*.)

Dame-oshi (dah-may-oh-she)—*Dame* by itself means something is "no good" or "bad" or "useless." With the addition of *oshi*, the term means "to make sure" or "to confirm." It is a very important word in doing business in Japan because it is expected and customary for people to reconfirm delivery or shipping dates, appointments, decisions, and so on (the implication being that circumstances may change unexpectedly).

Danketsu (don-kate-sue)—Literally "union" or "combination," this term is used in reference to the unity that the Japanese see as one of the primary sources of the energy they apply to business.

Danshi jugyo-in (dahn-she juu-ghee-yoe-een)—All the male employees below the rank of *kacho* (section chief).

Datsu-sara (dot-sue-sah-rah)—This literally means "to get away from a salary," and it refers to the recent trend for more and more younger and middle-aged Japanese salarymen to quit the corporations they work for and go out on their own—still an unconventional and controversial thing to do.

Dorai (doe-rye)—This is the English word *dry*. The Japanese adopted it to mean the kind of impersonal, profit-oriented approach to business attributed to Western businessmen. Conversely, their own *ninjo* (human feelings) oriented business system is regarded as "wet" ("wet-toe"). The same words are also applied to one's attitude toward the opposite sex.

Doru-bako (doe-rue-bah-koe)—Literally "dollarbox," which is a take-off on *kane-bako* (moneybox), this term is used in reference to a company's most profitable product, business line, or department. It is also used in reference to a financial backer, who becomes someone's *doru-bako*.

Dosa mawari (doe-sah mah-wah-ree)—Originally "touring around" and applied to theatrical troupes, *dosa mawari* now refers to an individual in a company who is rotated to two or more provincial offices or branches in succession (and is usually used in a negative sense). Since employees are seldom fired in Japan, head offices often assign undesirable individuals to branches or subsidiaries on a permanent basis, a process known as *tobasareta* (toe-bah-sah-ray-tah) (being kicked out).

Dosatsu ryoku   (doe-sot-sue ree-yoe-kuu)—Able to "see through things," to have "keen insight"; it is a quality the Japanese look for in a top executive.

Dososei   (doe-soh-say-ee)—Japanese businessmen probably do more networking than any other businessmen in the world, but they do it only within very specifically defined groups with which they have well-established bonds. Often the most important of these groups is their *dososei* or alumni brothers. A lot of business in Japan results only because individuals have alumni in other companies. When a Japanese begins to think about developing a relationship with another company, he is most likely to consider first whether or not he has an alumnus in the other firm. Foreign businessmen in Japan who are graduates of Japanese universities have a decided advantage in being able to count large numbers of Japanese businessmen as their "brothers."

Fuku shacho   (fuu-kuu shah-choe)—A *fuku shacho* is a vice-president, a title that is not very common in Japan. In Japanese companies, the role of the vice-president in the Western sense is more likely filled by a director.

Fundoshi hitotsu de   (foon-doe-she he-tote-sue day)—Literally, "with one *fundoshi.*" A *fundoshi* is a narrow loincloth and is the traditional Japanese equivalent of "shorts" or "panties" as the case may be. The phrase *fundoshi hitotsu de* is an old one and refers to starting a company or project with little or no capital—on a G-string instead of a shoestring.

Futokoro-gatana   (fuu-toe-koe-roe-gah-tah-nah)—Literally a "breast-dagger" (which in feudal Japan was the knife used by samurai to commit *hara-kiri*), the word is now used to refer to the "right-hand man" of a boss; one who is totally trusted and functions as an executive's chief of staff. The term is complimentary.

Gaijin   (guy-jeen)—An "outside person," this is the Japanese word for "foreigner." You hear it often in Japan because foreigners there, especially Caucasians, blacks, and browns, stick out like sore thumbs. The connotation of the word has long been derogatory, so speakers often add the word *kata,* very polite for "person," to it—*gaijin-no kata* or "foreign person."

Gashi-kokan (Gah-she-koe-khan)—*Gashi-kokan* are Happy New Year parties staged by industrial associations and other business organizations for several days after offices reopen following New Year's. The purpose of the parties is to make it convenient for businessmen to meet large numbers of their associates to wish everyone a Happy New Year and ask for their continued goodwill, cooperation, and business during the new year. *Gashi-kokan* (which are also called *meishi-kokan* or "exchanging business cards") are normally held during the day. They invariably involve numerous toasts with *sake* or beer, leaving the participants red-faced and sweating.

Gekokujo (gay-koe-kuu-joe)—"To go over the head of one's superior," something that in feudal days could result in one losing his head, literally. The practice is still very much frowned on in contemporary Japan and frequently acts as a barrier to business.

Go-en (go-inn)—The exclusive group-oriented nature of Japanese society makes it necessary for them to have *en* (relations) with an individual or company before they can do business with them. *En* is also the medium or cause that results in relations being established between groups. Two companies cannot engage in business without *en* having been established, and this necessary relationship cannot be established with a phone call. It requires introductions and a series of face-to-face meetings.

Goma-suri (go-mah-sue-ree)—As a society with a highly refined social etiquette and strict rules governing interpersonal relations, the Japanese have developed numerous techniques for smoothing human relations and making other people feel good. One of these techniques is known as *goma-suri,* which literally means "grinding sesame seeds" but is used figuratively to mean flattering someone. The Japanese often act embarrassed when paid compliments, but they themselves pay compliments at the drop of a single Japanese word or if you manage to put one bite of food into your mouth with chopsticks. Foreigners not used to the kind of effusive *goma-suri* practiced by the Japanese are often put off balance and made more vulnerable.

Goshugi torihiki (go-shuu-ghee toe-ree-he-kee)—*Shugi* means "celebration" or "congratulations" and *torihiki* means "business." Put together they refer to giving a company some business to help it celebrate a special occasion (like an opening or an anniversary or the first day of business after New Year's). This is a traditional and honored custom in Japan and is part of the Japanese way of incorporating a strongly personal element into their business practices.

Gote-ni mawaru (go-tay-nee ma-wah-rue)—Derived from the game of *go*, this figuratively means to get behind or be behind. In a business context it refers to letting your competitor or negotiating counterpart get one up on you.

Gyosei-shido (ghee-yoe-say-she-doe)—This is the famous (or infamous) "administrative guidance" of business practiced by bureaucrats in several key government ministries. The "guidance" consists of forcing or persuading businessmen to follow certain policies or guidelines that are not required by law but are believed by the bureaucrats to be in the interest of the country. The pressure the ministries can bring to bear on individual companies, as well as on industries, is enormous.

Hae-nuki (hie-nuu-kee)—The word for "true-born," *hae-nuki* refers to a person who entered a company right out of school and has never worked anywhere else, and it confers a special status upon individuals in that category. It ranges from difficult to impossible for a person who has worked elsewhere to join a new, large company and be fully accepted by *hae-nuki* employees.

Hakurai suhai (hah-kuu-rie sue-hie) Literally "the worship of foreign goods," this term is used in reference to the attraction that high-quality, famous name-brand imported goods have for the Japanese. The concept and the fascination go back to the mid-1850s, when Japan began trading with the West after more than 200 years of self-imposed isolation. A few Japanese still buy imported goods just because they are foreign, but most consumers consider quality and after-service first.

Hame wo hazusu (hah-may oh hah-zuu-suu)—Literally "pull out all of the stops," this term is in reference to "letting one's hair down" and engaging in unrestrained drinking and merrymaking at company parties and when out drinking with fellow workers at night. Anyone who does not or cannot *hame wo hazusu* is suspect in Japan. Such a person is likely to be regarded as unfriendly, arrogant, and hiding his real self.

Hanko (hahn-koe)—These are the "chops" or "seals" the Japanese use in lieu of their signature when signing documents or papers. There are three kinds of *hanko:* the *Jitsu-in,* or Registered Seal, for legal or official documents; the *Mitome-in,* or Private Seal, for everyday transactions, such as signing receipts or accepting registered mail and the like; and the *Ginko-in,* or Bank Seal, for bank transactions. Registered seals usually include the owner's full name, while the private ones usually have only the family name.

Since *hanko,* especially the *Jitsu-in,* represent the official signature of the owner, special care must be taken to ensure that they do not fall into the hands of anyone who would misuse them. The *hanko* are pressed first on a vermilion ink pad and then on the document. (In feudal Japan, only the samurai and aristocrats were allowed to use red ink. Commoners had to use black ink.)

Quite a few foreigners who are permanent residents of Japan have *hanko* made and registered.

Hara-gei (hah-rah-gay-ee)—*Hara-gei* is the art of doing business "from the stomach," because the Japanese traditionally believed that the stomach was the center of man's being and emotions. The word *hara* also appears in a number of other words and phrases that are regularly used in business: *hara wo miseru,* to show the stomach or reveal what is on one's mind; *hara wo watte hanasu,* to cut open the stomach or have a heart-to-heart talk; *hara wo kukuru,* to bundle up the stomach or become resolved to a situation and make the best of it; *hara ga tatsu,* the stomach stands up—i.e., to get angry; he is *hara-guroi* (he has a "black stomach"—i.e., is wicked, crafty). One who does business on *hara-gei* depends upon "gut feeling"— which is sometimes characterized as being subtle, devious, and/or cunning. The word is not used daily, but the practice is common.

Hashigo-zake (hah-she-go-zah-kay)—It is a deeply entrenched custom for Japanese office workers, especially those who have started up the rungs of the corporate promotional ladder, to go out in groups after work to drink, relax, get to know one another, air grievances, and otherwise blow off steam that builds up during the day. The group usually goes to several drinking places, getting "higher" as they go along—a process popularly known as *hashigo-zake* or *hashigo-nomi*, literally "ladder drinking." Because the Japanese are conditioned not to reveal their true thoughts and character while sober and on the job, these institutionalized evening drinking bouts in bars and cabarets serve as an important adjunct to communication and maintaining good personal relations within companies.

Hatarakibachi (hah-tah-rah-kee-bah-chee)—This is the Japanese word for workaholic. It is not heard as often as one might expect, perhaps because everyone is expected to work hard.

Hataraku (hah-tah-rah-kuu)—This is the word for work. It is made up of compounds that mean "give rest to other people." The root meaning of *hataraku* implies that the Japanese regard work as a service to others, as opposed to a task they perform for their own personal benefit.

Hijikake-isu (he-jee-kah-kay-ee-sue)—It is usually impossible to spot the managers in a Japanese office by their chairs. As soon as a person is promoted to *kakaricho*, the first rung on the managerial ladder, he moves up to an armchair. The higher he goes up the executive ladder, the larger and more comfortable his chair. Directors and presidents usually have *hijikake-isu* (armrest chairs), leather-upholstered chairs that are for sitting in and thinking rather than working in.

Hi-no-kuruma (he-no-kuu-rue-mah)—When people or companies in Japan suffer from financial difficulties, they are said to be on a *hi-no-kuruma,* or "fire car" (or cart), which is the vehicle used in Buddhist hell to transport dead sinners.

Hiru andon (he-rue on-doan)—In the typical Japanese corporation, presidents, general managers, and department heads often play only a minor role in day-to-day management, leaving that to their deputies or assistants. These "symbolic" heads are sometimes referred to as *hiru andon,* or "day lamps," the idea being that you cannot tell whether or not a light is turned on during daylight hours. Such people often appear to have no duties or obligations, and it does not seem to make any difference whether or not they are there. The Japanese have traditionally preferred this system as part of management by consensus.

Hito hada nugu (he-toe hah-dah nuu-guu)—Literally, "to remove one layer of skin." Figuratively, it means to do someone a favor without expecting anything in return or to repay a past favor (reluctantly).

Hitori-zumo (he-toe-ree-zuu-moe)—Sumo wrestling is Japan's traditional national sport. *Hitori-zumo* is a "one-man sumo match." It refers to an individual who takes on a very difficult task by himself, without getting anyone to help him, and who ends up running around in circles, working very hard, but failing. Foreigners who are not familiar with the group approach in Japan often try to persuade individuals in Japanese companies to take on products or programs as their own personal projects without realizing they are asking the people to engage in *hitori-zumo.*

Hiya-meshi-kui (he-yah-may-she-kuu-ee)—In a business or government office context, a person who has been made into a *hiya-meshi-kui,* or "cold-rice-eater," has been shuffled aside into a powerless, meaningless position. People who have been pushed back or off the promotional ladder often complain of being forced to eat *hiya-meshi.* Foreign businessmen who approach Japanese companies without impressive introductions and advance preparations are sometimes shuffled off onto *hiya-meshi-kue.*

Ho-toku (hoe-toe-kuu)—Perhaps more than any other people, the Japanese are imbued with a sense of *toku,* or virtue, which traditionally has been a part of their religious and educational upbringing. In addition to contributing to their sense of Japaneseness and nationhood, this conditioning has also helped shape their sense of social and economic obligation and is responsible in part for their cooperative approach to life, to the low level of violence in the country, etc. Instruction in virtue was an integral part of life in feudal Japan.

After the feudal system officially ended in 1868, the teaching of virtue was incorporated into the educational curriculum, and *Ho-toku,* or "The Way of Virtue," societies were formed. The "way of virtue" is still important in the making of the Japanese.

Insei (inn-say-ee)—In old Japan *insei* referred to the system under which an emperor retired but continued to rule from behind the scenes. Nowadays it refers to a businessman or politician who has retired but continues to exercise authority and power in his former company or organization. The situation is very common, especially in politics and in companies where the retiree is the founder. A similar term is *O-gosho,* which originally meant the residence of a retired *shogun* (military dictator). Today it refers to the most prominent and powerful individual ("the grand old man") in any area of endeavor, including business, politics, the arts, etc.

Ippai yarimasho (eep-pie yah-ree-mah-show)—This literally means "let's fill the stomach," but in usage it means "let's go have a drink," with it understood that the person making the suggestion wants to talk to the other person privately and/ or frankly, or wants to develop a closer relationship with the individual or show appreciation, etc. In other words, the person making such an invitation usually always has some purpose beyond just relaxing and drinking. (See also *chotto ippai.*).

Iro-ke (ee-roe-kay)—By itself *iro* means "color" and by extension, "sex," "love," and "desire" or "interest." *Ke* means more or less "slight tinge." When attached to *iro,* the combination means a tinge of sexual awareness or interest. A businessman who shows some interest in an idea or project may be described as *iro-ke wo misete-iru,* or showing signs of interest. Anyone who wants something badly is often described as *iro-ke tappuri,* or "full of desire."

Iro wo tsukeru (ee-roe oh t'sue-kay-rue)—This basically means "to apply color" and is used to mean "give special consideration to" or to "fix up" or take care of or do something for somebody. It is often used in business in reference to negotiations or wage bargaining, when one side volunteers to add a little extra to the arrangement. In colloquial usage, *iro* means sexually attractive. An *iro-otoko* is a handsome (sexy)·

man. When used by itself, *iro* can mean lover or sweetheart.

Isekki mokeru (ee-say-kee moe-kay-rue)—To take someone to a bar, restaurant, geisha house, etc., in order to get on
friendly terms prior to discussing business—the word is ar-
chaic, but the practice is very up-to-date.

Ishin denshin (ee-sheen dane-sheen)—This is usually
translated as "tacit understanding" or "telepathy," and it is
used in reference to nonverbal communication, a very important part of both social and business intercourse in Japan. As
an ancient, sophisticated culture with a detailed and highly
stylized etiquette, the Japanese are very sensitive to nonverbal
communication, ranging from the well-known bow to the
action of leaning back, closing their eyes, and appearing to be
dozing or at least paying no attention during business negotiations. They *are* resting, but they are also thinking about what
has been said, planning what to say next, etc. The uninitiated
Western businessman is likely to become frustrated and possibly angered by such behavior. The literal meaning of *ishin
denshin* is "what the mind thinks, the heart transmits."

Jibara wo kiru (jee-bah-rah oh kee-rue)—This literally
means "to cut one's own stomach," but it does not refer to the
form of ritual suicide practiced in feudal Japan. Instead, it
refers to a boss or manager paying for nighttime entertainment for his subordinates with his own money (as opposed to
a company allowance). The purpose behind this ritual practice is to promote goodwill, cooperation, and loyalty among
groups that work together in companies.

Jihyo (jee-h'yoe)—It is almost as difficult to quit a major
Japanese company as it is to be employed by one. The individual who wants to resign or quit must submit a formal letter
called *jihyo,* which the company may or may not accept. The
company has no legal hold over an employee but can bring
considerable pressure against anyone wanting to leave. A
firm's efforts to prevent an employee from leaving may have
nothing to do with his abilities or real value. The effort may
be, and often is, based on the desire to maintain the integrity
and continuity of the lifetime employment system and to
prevent the practice of leaving one firm for another from
becoming common. If a company does not accept a *jihyo* and

the individual leaves anyway, it becomes a serious black mark in his record that might later haunt him. If the resignation is accepted, however, it becomes an *en-man-taisha,* or "harmonious retirement."

Jingi wo kiru (jeen-ghee oh kee-rue)—Altogether, *jingi* means "humanity-benevolence-justice-righteousness," regarded in Confucian terms as the basic principles of morality. In feudal Japan *jingi* became the ethical code of the samurai and was eventually taken over by the *yakuza,* Japan's organized crime groups, which made it the basis for the relationship between gang leaders and their followers. The *yakuza* began using the phrase *jingi wo kiru* (to cut *jingi*) to describe the distinctive way they introduce themselves (with special gestures and facial expressions). Nowadays, companies planning on introducing a new product line in competition with other companies already in the field will go to these companies and *jingi wo kiri*—that is, introduce themselves and say they want to cooperate to avoid excessive competition. Companies will also make such introductory visits to other firms in the same line of business when they entice employees away from them. When used by businessmen in these circumstances, the phrase has a negative feeling, since it describes an obligation that can be very unpleasant.

Jinji-ido (jeen-jee-e-doe)—Every year in March (just before the end of the fiscal year for most companies), Japanese corporations transfer dozens to hundreds of their employees from one department or division to another in an ongoing process to give them as much experience as possible. This particularly applies to those being groomed as managers. Companies whose fiscal year ends in December usually conduct their *jinji-ido* (personnel transfers) in October. Managerial candidates who have reached the age at which a promotion is in order are especially anxious about the *jinji-ido* because their new post will tell them if they are still on track or if they are being shuffled aside to posts that are off the main line. The custom of *jinji-ido* is of specific interest to foreign businessmen dealing with Japanese companies because it means that every few years their key contacts are changed. This means they have to repeatedly go through the process of getting acquainted with new submanagers and managers and developing good relations with them. It is especially important to keep this in mind during the spring months and in the fall, just before and just after the *jinji-ido* takes place. Foreign businessmen frequently find themselves in the position of having started a project with a group of people only to find they face an entirely new group, sometimes while the project is being negotiated.

Jin-myaku (jeen-me-yah-kuu)—This literally means the "pulse of a human being," man or a person, but it is used in the sense of personal connections, with the connotation being that good business (or personal) relations depends on having good personal contacts. Generally speaking, the Japanese will not engage in business with anyone from another company unless he or she has been introduced to them by one of their *jin-myaku* (personal connections). It is often said that the biggest asset a businessman can have in Japan is a wide circle of *jin-myaku*. The foreign businessman who wants to succeed in Japan must also develop his own circle of personal connections and must work constantly to keep them alive and well.

Jirei (jee-ray)—This is the official document that the personnel departments of larger companies and government bureaus issue to individuals to inform them that they have been hired, transferred, reassigned, retired, or fired. Once a *jirei* has been issued, there is generally no appeal, no matter how upsetting or unfair it might seem to an employee. *Jirei* are normally issued in the spring, when the companies and government bureaus take in batches of just-graduated college students. In the case of ranking corporation executives or government officials, news of appointments and dismissals are sometimes leaked to newspapers, in which case they are known as *shimbun* (newspaper) *jirei,* and are not necessarily final. The spring season is understandably a period of tension and fear for many Japanese workers.

Joshi jugyo-in (joe-she juu-ghee-yoe-een)—The female employees of a company. It is still rare to find women in management positions in major Japanese companies. The most common exceptions are found in the service industries.

Kaigi (kie-ghee)—A meeting, or conference, of which there are many kinds in Japan. In their meetings, particularly for the purpose of negotiating business arrangements, the Japanese seem to be most comfortable with groups of about ten persons, with each allowed to have his say. Such meetings most often start out in a relaxed, informal way. Their custom of discussing every possibility, and repeating the same questions in slightly different ways, often results in talks going on for days or weeks—and sometimes for months. Meetings play a decisive role in the consensus aproach to decisions.

Kaki-ire-doki (kah-kee-ee-ray-doe-kee)—The literal meaning of this term is "time to write in" (sales entries or items put up for collateral), but it is now used to mean "the most profitable time" and refers to the major sales periods in department stores and other retailers (especially the two major gift-buying seasons, *ochugen* [o-chu-gain] in midsummer and *oseibo* [o-say-e-boe] in December), as well as the best sales periods of manufacturers and other businesses. When negotiating deals with Japanese companies, it is often helpful to know their *kaki-ire-doki*.

Kakushi-gei (kah-kuu-she-gay-ee)—Literally "hidden art," *kakushi-gei* refers to a special skill or talent that one has practiced in secret so as to be able to put on a good show when called upon to perform in public—which the Japanese are often required to do. The most common *kakushi-gei* are singing and folk dancing, but they might be acrobatics, mime, imitations, or some other skill that can be performed before an audience. Another word for *kakushi-gei* is *ohako*, which means *juhachi-ban* or "number eighteen" and refers to the eighteen best plays of the legendary Ichikawa family of *kabuki* actors. The word is read as *hako*, meaning box, apparently because the Ichikawa's kept the manuscripts of the eighteen plays in a safety box.

Kami (kah-me)—This is the word for "god" (usually written with a small *g*), which is synonymous with divine spirit and, in ordinary usage, with "the greatest" or "the best." Individuals who are regarded as the best in their field are often referred to as "the god of sales," "the god of baseball," "the god of movie-making," etc.

Kanban (kahn-bahn)—In ordinary usage *kanban* means

"sign" or "bulletin board," but in business it has come to mean "just in time parts delivery," a management technique that was pioneered by Sakichi Toyoda, founder of Toyoda Automatic Loom Works Ltd., the predecessor of Toyota Motor Corporation, in the 1920s and continued by his son and successor Kiichiro Toyoda in the 1930s. The process was perfected in the years following the end of World War II (1945) by Taiichi Ono, manager (and later vice-president) of Toyota Motor Company Ltd., which had replaced Toyoda Automatic Loom Works Ltd. In 1978 Ono wrote a book describing the "just in time" system: *Toyota Seisan Hoshiki* (*The Toyota System of Production*), which was published by Diamond. The use of the word *kanban* grew out of the fact that every morning Toyoda would put a list of all the parts and supplies that would be needed for the day on a big bulletin board on the floor of his loom factory.

Kangaete okimasu   (kahn-guy-eh-tay oh-kee-mahss)—This literally means "I will think about it," but when a Japanese businessman says it to you following some kind of approach or presentation, it invariably means no.

Kangei kai   (kahn-gay kie)—*Kangei kai,* or "Welcome parties," are an important part of employee relations in Japanese companies. *Kangei kai* are held when new employees enter a company, when individuals are assigned to new departments, when staff members return from overseas assignments, and various other occasions. Such parties are marked by drinking, eating, and merrymaking, and are aimed at developing and strengthening group identity and loyalty. (See also *Sobetsu kai.*)

Kanri shoku   (kahn-ree show-kuu)—There is much less distinction between the *kanri shoku* or "managerial level" and ordinary workers in Japanese companies. Lower and middle-level managers generally do not have private offices or secretaries; all employees usually dress alike, eat in the same place, and in general are indistinguishable from staff members except for age and seating arrangement. Managers sit at the "head" of rows of desks. The oldest man in the office is usually the ranking individual.

Kanryo shugi   (kahn-rio shuu-ghee)—A term referring to

the attitudes and manners associated with bureaucrats, i.e., "bureaucratic."

Kao (kah-oh)—Besides the deeply felt need of the Japanese to *kao tateru* (save face), "face" is very important in other business contexts. A person who is well known and has many business contacts is one whose *kao ga hiroi* (face is wide). The person who has many contacts must work to keep them fresh and strong and spends a lot of time *kao wo tsunagu* (tying up or fastening his face). If someone says *kao wo kashite* (lend me your face) it means he wants to talk to you.

Kara-oke (kah-rah-oh-kay)—Literally "empty orchestra," *kara-oke* is a type of singing into a microphone hooked up to speakers in concert with recorded orchestra music. The singer thus sings along with the "orchestra." *Kara-oke* singing became popular in Japan in the 1970s, and quickly spread to the bars and lounges where businessmen gather by the hundreds of thousands each night after work. A significant percentage of Japanese businessmen regularly patronize *kara-oke* bars and take pride in their ability to belt out several songs, often in English as well as Japanese. The foreign visitor to Japan who wants to develop deep rapport with his Japanese colleagues will come prepared to take his turn when invited to such bars.

Kasei (kah-say-ee)—This is the "section system" which is the organizational basis for virtually all Japanese companies. The basic unit in companies is the section (*ka*), next is a department or division (*bu*). The manager of a section is a *kacho*. The assistant manager is a *kakaricho*). The manager of a department or division is a *bucho*. There may be only two or three people in a section of a small company and a dozen or more in larger companies. A department will be made up of several sections. In many ways, the *kacho* are the most important people in a Japanese company. Most plans and projects originate in the *ka*, and virtually all staff work is accomplished under the direction of the *kacho*. On the other hand, *bucho* spend most of their time chairing or attending intradepartment or division meetings. In larger companies *bucho* are the equivalent of vice-presidents in Western firms as far as rank and privilege are concerned, but they are generally not directly involved in creating or implementing programs, leaving that up to the *kakaricho* and *kacho*. Perhaps the most telling difference between the activities and responsibilities of Japanese *bucho* and American or European vice-presidents is that the *bucho* almost never have secretaries (since they don't do anything that make them necessary or useful).

Kayui tokoro ni te ga todoku   (kah-yuu-ee toe-koe-roe nee tay gah toe-doe-kuu)—Japanese hotels, shops, and other places of business are rightfully famous for the variety and degree of service they provide to their customers. The degree and importance of this service are emphasized by the phrase *kayui tokoro ni te ga todoku,* which means "to scratch where it itches." The implication is that few things feel better than for someone to scratch you in an itchy place that you can't reach, and that it is up to people in business, especially those in the service industry, to know exactly where, when, and how to "scratch" customers to please them the most.

Keibatsu   (kay-ee-bot-sue)—*Batsu* means "group," "faction," or "clique," and it is a very important word in the businessman's vocabulary, since most individuals and companies are members of and work within specific groups as teams. Virtually all activity in larger Japanese companies is on a group basis. *Kei* refers to "family" and, when used in combination with *batsu,* has the meaning of nepotism or family ties. Family ties and connections play a vital role in getting employment in the most desirable companies and government ministries and in rising in the social and political hierarchies. Most Japanese do not feel secure except as members of a group, and individually they are often unable to cope with conflicting situations. As part of this insecurity, most Japanese have difficulty accepting personal criticism. They are inclined to take such criticism as hostile, and aimed at all Japanese, not just themselves.

Keiko   (kay-ee-koe)—A term that used to mean "studying" or "considering old things," *keiko* is now used in reference to studying traditional artistic or martial arts skills, such as flower arranging, playing the *koto,* or practicing judo or fencing. Learning how to sing is also regarded as *keiko.* Most larger Japanese companies offer various *keiko* to their employees.

Keiretsu kaisha (kay-rate-sue kie-shah)—*Keiretsu* means "affiliated" or "series," and *kaisha* means "company." This term refers to the grouping of companies in Japan, including parent companies, subsidiaries, and subcontract firms, as well as those grouped around a certain bank or trading company. The system is an outgrowth of the economic structure of feudal Japan, when older employees of businesses were allowed to go out and establish their own companies while maintaining close ties with their former employers. Members of specific company groups cooperate with one another in various ways, in what often amounts to an exclusive network. The group a particular company "belongs to" can be a vital factor in its dealings with foreign companies.

Kenami ga yoi (kay-nah-me gah yoe-ee)—Literally, "good stock," as in a dog or horse with good bloodlines, but also it is frequently used in reference to a person who has a good family and educational background.

Kessai-ken (kace-sie-ken)—This is the authority under which a ranking executive approves of a *ringi-sho* proposal, thereby permitting his subordinates to take whatever action the document calls for. Approving a *ringi-sho* does not mean, however, that the ranking executive is responsible for the results of the policy or project if it fails. Responsibility falls on all of the managers who stamped the proposal.

Kiboh-taishoku (kee-boh-tie-show-kuu)—This is "compulsory retirement," a system that exists in most Japanese companies practicing lifelong employment. The compulsory retirement age ranges from fifty-five to sixty for most employees. Interestingly enough *kibo* means "with hope" with the obvious connotation being that the retiree "hopes" he will survive to enjoy his retirement. Employees who retire receive a lump sum of money based on their length of service and basic wage. Employees who retire before reaching the official retirement age receive considerably less in retirement benefits.

Kimochi no shirushi (kee-moe-chee no she-rue-she)—*Kimochi* means "feeling" and *shirushi* means "sign" or "evidence." Put together, they refer to the small gifts Japanese businessmen and others carry with them on trips abroad to give to people who befriend them. Businessmen making long trips abroad and calling on lots of people may carry three or four dozen *kimochi no shirushi* in their luggage. Foreign businessmen visiting Japan are not automatically expected to follow the same custom, but it is advisable since it demonstrates both an awareness of Japanese customs and sincerity in establishing the "right kind" of ties with your Japanese counterparts.

Kimon (kee-moan)—This word originally meant "devil gate" and referred to a gate or door on the northeast corner of a home or building (through which devils were likely to enter, since devils were believed to come from the northeast). Now it is used in reference to a person who is hard to get along with, in the sense of one's personal nemesis. It is used in business when someone finds he or she cannot get along with a member of another group or someone in another company. The person will say, "So-and-so is my *kimon*. Have somebody else go see him." A *kimon* may also be a thing that causes you a lot of trouble, like keeping track of your traveling expenses.

Kone (koe-nay)—Short for "connections" or "personal connections" through family or school ties, etc., it is a very important asset in Japan's business world.

Konjo (kone-joe)—If a foreign businessman in Japan wants to hire a Japanese salesman or manager, he should find out if the prospect has *konjo*, which means "fighting spirit." By the same token, a foreigner who is negotiating with the Japanese has his work cut out for him if his Japanese counterpart is a *konjo ga aru otoko* (man with fighting spirit). Such men are noted for never letting adversity get them down, never giving up no matter what the odds. In fact, the more resistance they meet, the harder they fight.

Kubi (kuu-bee)—In a country where decapitation by sword was a common form of punishment for many centuries, reference to one's neck was especially meaningful. The term is still used in many key expressions. Some of them: *kubi wo kakete*, stake my neck; *kubi wo kiru*, to cut the neck or fire someone; *kubi wo tobu*, the neck/head flies off, also refers to letting someone go; *kubi ga mawaranai*, neck/head will not turn, said when a person or company is in debt and cannot do much about it; *mawata kubi wo shimeru,* literally to strangle someone with a silken thread, or to make conditions so difficult for a person that he will leave a company on his own.

Kuromaku (kuu-roe-mah-kuu)—In politics as well as in many industries in Japan, there are usually one or more *kuromaku* or very influential men who have no official office but who exercise decisive power and control most important events. It is often necessary to get the approval and cooperation of these men in political and business situations. The term *kuromaki* means "black curtain" and comes from the theater (where it hid those pulling the strings of puppets, etc.).

Mae-daoshi (my-dah-oh-she)—Literally "front-loading" (and referring to standing streetcar passengers falling forward when the conductor suddenly brakes), *mae-daoshi* is used in a business context to refer to advancing the schedule of a project. The inference is that everyone must make a special effort to move forward together in order for the project to succeed.

Mae muki ni kangaete okimasu (My muu-kee nee khan-guy-eh-tay oh-kee-mahss)—*Mae muki ni* means "in the forward direction" and, when preceding *kangaete okimasu,* it means something like "I will give it (your proposition) some thought with the (slight) possibility of moving forward on it." (See also *Kangaete okimasu.*)

Mago-koro (mah-go-koe-roe)—This is translated as "true heart" or "sincerity," and is a very important factor in all relations in Japan. The businessman in particular expects all of his suppliers and customers to conduct themselves with honesty and integrity, and he is concerned about starting any business with a new company until he is satisfied that his counterparts in the company can be trusted to behave with sincerity and "true heart."

Meibutsu (may-ee-boot-sue)—"Famous product." Practically every region or prefecture in Japan has been noted for centuries for one or more of its distinctive products. Always popular with travelers, some of these *meibutsu* are now distributed nationally. Also, *meibutsu otoko* means "outstanding man."

Meiwaku (may-ee-wah-kuu)—Literally "annoyance" or "trouble," this word is frequently used in the sense of an apology. In Japan the formal apology generally includes humbling oneself, accepting responsibility, and often making restitution in the form of cash payments for damages, mental suffering, sickness, etc.

Mekura-ban (may-kuu-rah-bahn)—By itself *mekura* means "blind." *Ban* means "watchman" or "guard." In combination they refer to an executive stamping his name-seal (*hanko*) on a *ringi-sho* without reading it.

Miso (me-soe)—A salty paste made from soybeans, *miso* is one of the two primary food flavorings (the other is soybean sauce) of Japanese cuisine and represents the essence of the "Japanese" taste. In business the term is used either to mean a "good" or "advantagous point" or to refer to a blunder of some kind. A product without *miso* has no good points; a product with *miso* has something special about it that makes it easier to sell. Businesses without *miso* are in for a hard time. To put *miso* on something, negotiations or whatever, is not a good thing to do (because *miso* looks like some kind of dirty mess).

Myaku (me-yah-ku)—This is an important word in Japan's business lexicon because it means the "pulse-beat" and is used in reference to many areas of business—how a presentation is going, how a project is going, etc., in the sense that it is a barometer of business. Japanese businessmen "read the pulse" of a business project by accumulating and analyzing bits of information from as many sources as possible—a process that can be long and tedious to a foreign contact.

Naikei (nie-kay-ee)—"Unwritten rules," usually referring to various practices followed by lower ranking bureaucrats in the Ministry of International Trade and Industry and the Finance Ministry, which often go beyond the laws the ministries are supposed to enforce. These bureaucrats see themselves as Japan's last line of defense against encroachments by foreign businesses into the country.

Najimi (nah-jee-mee)—Japanese businessmen make a special point of meeting and developing friendly relations with managers of restaurants and clubs (and club hostesses) where they go for their own enjoyment as well as for entertaining customers. The aim is to make sure they get good treatment and (in bars and clubs) are not overcharged. A frequent restaurant or cabaret patron is known as an *O-najimi*. If you are the *najimi* of a cabaret hostess, you are a good and favored customer. Having *najimi* in bars and restaurants around town gives you "face." In retail shops, department stores, and other kinds of businesses, a good customer is known as *tokui* (toe-kuu-e) and always gets special attention.

Nakama (nah-kah-mah)—*Nakama* may mean either "companion" or "group," and it is symbolic of the close personal relationship that must exist among Japanese employees for them to function effectively. The term includes connotations of cooperation, conformity, and similarity in thought and behavior, along with the kinds of ties that bind blood brothers.

Nakatta koto ni suru (nah-kaht-tah koe-toe nee suu-rue)—This is a term that is often used in Japan in both personal and business situations. It figuratively means "wiping the slate clean" as far as a promise or commitment is concerned—to proceed as if the commitment were not made in the first place. In the case of business where a signed contract is concerned, a penalty may be paid. Even when a penalty is paid and there is agreement between the two parties that it is over, it does not always relieve the paying party from further obligation. The Japanese often ask for a *nakatta koto ni suru* when a situation becomes untenable.

Naruhodo (nah-rue-hoe-doe)—In ordinary conversation between people on the same social or professional level, this is a simple word meaning "Is that right! I now (finally) understand. I see. Indeed . . . " and more or less gives the impression that you agree with whatever the person is saying. It is regarded as impolite for juniors to use the term to seniors. In business, the term is used in the ordinary way, as well as in a formal way, to end discussions or negotiations when one party does not want to make a commitment and does not want to continue the meeting. In this case it is usually expressed as *"Naruhodo. Yoku wakarimashita. Yoku kento shite mimasu"* ("I see. I understand the matter very well and will give it serious study"). Foreign businessmen who continue to talk and push after the Japanese use this phrase are not only wasting everyone's time, they may seriously damage their case.

Nawabari (nah-wah-bah-ree) — An old term that referred to a maze of roped-off paths leading into a feudal castle, this term is now used in the sense of "home ground" or "territory" when office workers go out at night to drink at several bars (*hashigo-nomi*). One of the members of the party may say, "This is my *nawabari* (a bar that he frequents often), so everything is on me." It is a way of gaining and keeping "face" at the bar and obligating his friends to him.

Nenkin seido (nane-keen say-ee-doe) — "Pension system," something that is of growing importance to Japanese workers.

Newaza-shi (nay-wah-zah-she) — A *newaza-shi* is a person who is especially clever at behind-the-scene negotiations and who has built up a reputation for being able to do the impossible, usually by pulling some kind of surprise out of his bag. The term comes from the world of judo, where it refers to lying on the mat without moving, and suddenly executing an attack (*newaza*) from that position.

Nigiri tsubusu (nee-ghee-ree t'sue-buu-suu) — This literally means "to crush by hand," and it refers to a manager pigeonholing a written proposal passed to him by a subordinate. When this happens, the junior employee either forgets the proposal or takes a big chance and goes over his boss's head with a *jiki-so*, or "direct appeal." In the old days, when an underling went over the head of his feudal lord, he often forfeited his life and sometimes the lives of his family as well. In Japan's business world today, the man who resorts to a *jiki-so* might jeopardize his whole career if he does not have the support of other strong managers in the company. At the same time, if the *jiki-so* turns out to be accepted by higher-level management, the man who "crushed" it may be the loser.

Nippachi (neep-pah-chee) — Actually this is two words, *ni* (two) and *hachi* (eight), referring to February and August. When combined, the two words are pronounced as *nippachi* and refer to the fact that business is usually at its slowest and lowest in February and August. Because of this, many companies encourage their employees to take their vacations in August. Some companies close down for a week or so during August. A negative aspect of *nippachi* is that businessmen often use it as an excuse to put off commitments or paying bills for an additional month.

Nuke gake (nuu-kay gah-kay) — Another old term that originally referred to a warrior who would steal away from his camp and rush out to meet the enemy first, killing as many as possible in a surprise raid, *nuke gake* is now used in business in reference to an individual who attempts to "steal a march" on his colleagues and achieve some kind of major coup before anyone else in the company knows what he is doing. The rare man who succeeds in such a *nuke gake* may receive high praise from some of his superiors, but inevitably he is criticized by his colleagues and may endanger his relations with them for the rest of his working life.

Oitsuke! Oikose! (Oh-e-t'sue-kay! Oh-e-koe-say!) — When Japan opened its doors to the West in the mid-1850s, a slogan that soon became popular was "*Oitsuke! Oikose!*" which means "Catch up with the West! Pass the West!" The Japanese took the slogan very seriously.

O-mono (oh-moe-no) — Literally a "big thing," *O-mono* means an outstanding leader or "big shot" who is a boss but does not manage directly; one who commands such respect that his wishes are carried out without his giving orders. *O-mono* are highly regarded in Japan, and there are always a number of them in business, politics, and in other professions. The *O-mono* is very wise but often appears simple and even foolish in order not to appear arrogant to his employees or followers. True *O-mono* delegate authority but always take full responsibility for the actions of their underlings.

Onjin (own-jeen) — "Obligation person," or a person who helps another in some important area, such as getting into a choice school or company. The *onjin* is thereafter "responsible" for the person helped and may act as a go-between in matters relating to him or her. The person receiving the help is also obligated to the *onjin* for life.

O'rei   (oh-ray-ee)—The etiquette that requires all debts and favors to be acknowledged and paid for by bowing, expressing thanks, giving gifts, etc.—it is a vital part of social responsibility in Japan.

Otoko ga tatanai   (oh-toe-koe gah tah-tah-nie) — "My manhood won't stand up!" This is a phrase often used by a man (usually young) when pleading that he be allowed to assume a certain responsibility or be given a certain task, for the sake of his "manly honor."

Rikutsu-poi   (ree-kute-sue-poy) — *Rikutsu* means "logical" or "reasonable"; *poi* means "in excess" or "to have too much of." A person who is *rikutsu-poi* is too logical, too reasonable; not human enough; ignores the emotional side of things. The Japanese consider most foreigners, especially Americans, as *rikutsu-poi* and, therefore, difficult or impossible to get along with. Since Americans in particular pride themselves on being logical and reasonable, there is often a fundamental conflict when Japanese and Americans meet. When an American businessman negotiating with the Japanese runs into resistance, his natural tendency is to try to carry the day with pure logic and reasonableness. He is often surprised, shocked, and upset when it doesn't go over.

Saji wo nageru   (sah-jee oh nah-gay-rue) — In Japan one does not "throw in the towel"; he "throws in the spoon" — which is what many foreign businessmen do when they come up against the negotiating and business techniques employed by the Japanese.

Sasen   (sah-sen) — *Sasen* literally means "lowering the seating order," which harks back to Japan's feudal period when social and political position was often indicated by where the individual was seated when in attendance on his feudal lord, the Shogun, or members of the Imperial family. Today it is said to be one of the most feared words in the vocabulary of a Japanese manager because it refers to being demoted, either by being put into a situation where he has fewer people—or no one at all—working under him, or by being transferred from the parent company to a subsidiary without being promoted to a higher rank.

Seijitsu (say-ee-jeet-sue) — *Seijitsu* means "sincerity" with a Japanese flavor, of course, meaning that the word has a much broader and deeper use in Japan than elsewhere. The Japanese regard sincerity as the foundation of trust, and trust as the foundation for all business dealings—again within the cultural context of Japan. Americans, for example, will do business with the devil if he offers a good product or a good price. The Japanese give sincerity and trust precedence over product or price and will refuse to do business with companies whose management does not pass their sincerity/trust test.

Senjitsu wa domo arigato gozaimasu (sane-jeet-sue wah doe-moe ah-ree-gah-toe go-zie-mahss) — This is another institutionalized phrase, ritualistically repeated, that plays a key role in Japanese manners and ethics. It means "Thank you for the other day," and is said the next time you meet your benefactor after you have been treated to a dinner or lunch and/or a night on the town. By repeating this phrase, you acknowledge that you are indebted to your host for his hospitality and expect to reciprocate in the future (not necessarily by taking him out). If any business "understanding" was achieved during the eating or drinking bout, this is also the standard phrase to express gratitude.

Sensei (sane-say-ee) — This is the word for "teacher" and is used to address teachers and other professionals, such as lawyers as well as individuals who are highly accomplished in some field. When used in the usual way, it is a term of respect, but it may also be used behind someone's back in a derogatory sense or to his or her face as a bit of flattery or even a friendly insult. The Japanese will frequently address foreigners as *sensei* as a sign of respect. Some also use it as a way of flattering and softening up foreigners who are not familiar with the various uses and nuances of the word.

Sente wo utsu (sane-tay oh uut-sue) — Derived from the Japanese game of *Go,* which is similar to chess and very popular with businessmen, this phrase means to make a move that forces an opponent into an untenable position where he has to move in your favor. It has the connotation of "being ahead of the game" and is used in reference to business negotiations and other situations.

Senyu koraku (sen-yuu koe-rah-kuu) — Literally "Struggle first; enjoy later," this is a slogan that emphasizes the traditional work ethic of the Japanese. It is still a valid factor in Japan's economy, particularly in the number of hours many Japanese work without being paid overtime, and the fact that a significant percentage of the workers, especially on the managerial level, do not take all of the annual holidays they have coming.

Sha-fu (shah-fuu) — *Sha-fu* are the unwritten rules or codes of a company that apply to the conduct of employees, how they dress and behave to customers and the public, the image they present. It is also the corporate image of a company—how it is seen in the public eye—as conservative, innovative, progressive, and so on. Japanese companies are very sensitive about their *sha-fu*, and take great pains to mold new employees in the desired image. Once a company's image is damaged, by a scandal or for some other reason, it is very difficult to regain.

Shakun (shah-koon) — *Sha* means "company" and *kun* means "precepts." *Shakun* is the statement of a company's basic philosophy. The company "commandments," in other words. A similar word, *shaze*, more or less means "what is right for the company," and it is usually a statement of ideals or principles that is expressed in the form of a motto. Many companies have both *shakun* and *shaze*.

sha-nai (shah-nie) — This literally means "inside the company" and refers to the many activities within a Japanese company that are regarded as exclusive or private or confidential or for employees only. Each Japanese company is like an independent society, a community within itself, and things that are described as or labeled as *sha-nai* have more meaning than in the typical Western company. Among the *sha-nai* things in virtually all Japanese companies are *sha-nai ryoko*, company trips; *sha-nai kekkon*, company weddings; and *sha-nai yokin*, in-company savings.

Shintai ukagai (sheen-tie uu-kah-guy) — When an individual in a Japanese company makes a costly error or behaves in such a way that the company's reputation is harmed, he will often submit a *shintai ukagai*, or "informal resignation," acknowledging responsibility for the wrongdoing, expressing regret, and offering to resign. In the event that the individual refuses for some reason to submit such a resignation on his own, his superiors or colleagues may urge him to do so, knowing that if he voluntarily takes the step, company directors will be much more lenient and possibly let him off with only a token reprimand or minor punishment. In Japan an apology and expression of regret for misbehavior or a crime goes a long way toward expiating guilt. On the other hand, if someone is guilty of breaking the law or company rules and refuses to acknowledge responsibility or express regret, punishment can be very severe.

Shiri (she-ree) — The word means "butt," "rear end," "hips," or "ass," depending on the speaker's intent and tone of voice; and it is one of the most useful terms in the language. If someone is lazy or slow, he is *shiri ga omoi* (heavy assed). If someone really hustles, his *shiri ni hi ga tsuite imasu* (his butt is on fire). If you have to cover up for an incompetent colleague or *shiri nugui*, you "wipe his butt." If a woman is sexually loose, her *shiri ga karui* (she has a light butt). If a person is weak-minded and timid, his *shiri no ana ga chiisai* (he has a small asshole.).

Shita-uke (she-tah uu-kay) — A "subcontract firm," a company that depends on other firms, usually larger, for part or all of its business. Most name Japanese manufacturing companies use dozens to hundreds of *shita-uke,* many of which may be operated by former employees—a system that dates back centuries in Japan.

Shokuba no hana (show-kuu-bah no hah-nah) — "Flowers of the workplace" are young, usually attractive female office workers, who abound in Japan. The term has a double meaning. The women are pretty to look at and add a refreshing touch to the scene, but they are primarily just "wall flowers" who are not given any serious responsibility.

Shonen kyu (show-nane que) — The starting salary for new employees, it literally means "first-year income," which varies according to the size of the company, the educational level, etc.

Shuchu-go-uh (shuu-chuu-go-uh) — This is a peculiar word that means "downpour" or "torrentlike" as in a severe rainstorm. It is sometimes applied to Japan's "style of exporting," meaning that Japanese exporters often will totally flood a market with a particular product, virtually drowning all competition.

Shukko shain (shuke-koe shah-een) — *Shukko* means "to be on loan" and *sha* means "worker" or "employee"; so a *shukko shain* is one who is on loan to a subsidiary company or affiliated company. The word suggests that the employee will return to the parent or loaning company, but it often happens that the transfer is permanent, particularly when the parent company wants to get rid of the employee concerned. In most cases, employees on loan are selected because the subsidiary or connected company needs help in some specialized area, and since Japanese companies do not normally hire from the outside, someone from the parent company is dispatched to help them. It is common for banks to send *shukko shain* to companies that have huge loans outstanding and are having financial difficulties. The *shukko shain* system helps to bind parent and subsidiary companies as well as affiliated or aligned companies together, and is thus a part of the "business web" in Japan.

Shumu kisoku (shuu-mu kee-soe-kuu) — These are "rules of employment," something some Japanese workers have to read and sign when they are first hired. Employees of smaller companies are generally more interested in such rules than those who go to work for major corporations, feeling that they need the legal protection provided by the rules.

Shunto (shune-toe) — In 1955 Japan's major union federations devised a cooperative approach to helping workers in different industries gain annual wage increases. This new approach was labeled *Shunto*, which means "Spring Struggle." Several months prior to the annual *base-up* spring wage drive, labor leaders meet and decide on demands and possible strike tactics. Generally the unions have reached a concensus by January, and their coordinating committee announces the objectives of the forthcoming *Shunto*. Both management and unions are acutely aware of the damage caused by strikes and usually come to an agreement before the "Spring Struggle" occurs. When it is decided to strike, sometimes just as a show of force, the strikes are carefully orchestrated to last only an hour or so and are scheduled so that they cause as little disturbance as possible. For the last several years, the average Japanese worker has missed less than sixteen minutes of work per year as a result of strikes. The only unions in Japan that have staged prolonged strikes, for a week or longer, are generally those representing public workers.

Sobetsu kai (soe-bate-sue kie) — The *Sobetsu kai* is a "Farewell party," a very popular and common function in Japan, held when company employees are assigned overseas or to distant parts of the country, when someone is transferred from one department to another, when someone retires, etc. Sometimes farewell parties and welcome parties for new staff members, returning staff members, or replacements (*kangei kai*) are combined, in which case they are known as *kansogei kai*.

Soko wo nantoku (soe-koe oh nahn-toe-kuu) — If your Japanese counterpart gets a pained expression on his face and says, "Soko wo nantoku . . . " he is asking you to bend a little or give a little on a particular point, because he feels he has gone as far as he can and is giving a sign that he may not be able to accept the deal unless you do. If he adds *magete* (mah-gay-tay) or "bend" to the phrase ("*Soko wo magete nantoka* . . . "), the appeal is much stronger.

Soroban to awanai (so-roe-bahn toe ah-wah-nie) — Literally, "It doesn't agree with the abacus," this is an old term used to mean that the price is too high or that a business proposition would not be profitable. It is still used fairly often in informal, casual situations.

Taigu (tie-guu) — This word means "exceptionally good treatment, service, or entertainment" of the kind that is usually provided for people of high rank. A sumptuous dinner may be described as *taigu*. The word also appears on the name cards of individuals to indicate that they have the rank of department or division manager (or some other title) as far as salary and status are concerned, but no employees under them. The *taigu* title was devised to allow people with seniority to be promoted to higher ranks, even though there is no section or department for them to head.

Tamamushi (tah-mah-muu-she) — This is an insect that changes its color to fit its environment. A *tamamushi* contract or decision is one that changes with the viewpoint of the individuals involved. The contract or decision is worded in such a manner that it can be interpreted several different ways, and then the two sides "adjust" their behavior as they go along in order to make it work.

Tana ni ageru (tah-nah nee ah-gay-rue) — The Japanese are reluctant to say no outright, and they use a variety of subterfuges to avoid refusing and upsetting someone. One technique is to "accept" a proposal and then *tana ni ageru* (put it on the shelf). A shorter version of this, *tana-age*, is used when delaying a response or ignoring a matter entirely.

Tanshin funin-sha (tahn-sheen fuu-neen-shah) — This term literally means "one sent alone to a new assignment" and refers to the hundreds of thousands of Japanese men who each year are transferred by their parent companies to branches or subsidiaries in other parts of the country, without their families. These men are known in popular parlance as "business bachelors," and are both the brunt of jokes and the objects of a great deal of sympathy because of the hardships and inconvenience they must often endure, particularly those who are married. A few years ago a man who had been moved ten times by his company (Mitsubishi Trust & Banking Corporation) published a pamphlet titled "A Guidebook for Tanshin Funin-sha," which was distributed free to his fellow workers. One of the bits of advice in the booklet was, "Buy at least 20 sets of underwear."

Tarai-mawashi (tah-rie-mah-wah-she) — This is the proverbial "runaround," which is especially popular in Japan, particularly in government offices but also in business and other areas of life. The term *tarai-mawashi* refers to the stunt of lying on one's back and twirling a wooden washtub with the feet. When you go to government offices, especially to lodge a complaint, you are often sent from one section to another because no one wants to take responsibility for accepting or acting on your complaint. Foreign businessmen visiting Japanese companies without prior arrangement often feel like they are the victims of *tarai-mawashi* because they do not know which department to go to initially and are frequently shuffled around.

Tataki dai   (tah-tah-kee die)—*Tataki dai* literally means "a platform for pounding." It is used in business contexts to mean a suggestion or plan proposed by a lower ranking manager as a starting point for group discussions by all company executives concerned. If a consensus is reached, the plan may be adopted, the equivalent, you might say, of a verbal *ringi-sho*.

Teiki-saiyo   (tay-ee-kee-sie-yoe)—In April of each year, larger Japanese companies hire dozens to hundreds of new employees fresh out of high school and college in a system known as *teiki-saiyo*, or "periodic hiring." The bigger corporations do not hire for specific jobs but base the number of new recruits they take in each year on the natural attrition of their whole workforce, growth rate, and long-term strategic planning. The companies usually start the process in the fall of the previous year by inviting seniors in for unofficial interviews (see *aota-gai*). They are bound by an agreement not to start the screening or hiring process before October, but unofficially many of the more desirable students have jobs shortly after the beginning of the senior year. Examinations for company employment are held shortly after the first of each year. After entering their new company, the recruits are put through various training programs, including in some cases training retreats that are similar to military boot camps, where the training is not only intellectual and emotional but also physical.

Tei shisei   (tay she-say)—When things go wrong or when someone does not want to get involved or respond, it is common for them to *tei shisei*, or assume a "low posture," lay low, keep quiet, hoping that whatever it is will go away. It is as common in business as in private life, and it usually becomes apparent rather quickly.

Tonosama shobai   (toe-no-sah-mah show-buy)—In feudal

Japan the *tonosama* were clan lords (*daimyo*) who did not engage in business (*shobai*) but still had to deal with merchants in order to manage their fiefs, which basically were self-supporting domains. Having no experience in commercial affairs, and generally being arrogant and presumptuous because of their superior and privileged social rank, the *tonosama* were no match for the quick-witted merchants of Osaka, Nagoya, Edo (Tokyo), and other commercial centers in Japan. Today, companies that made it big in earlier times and make no serious effort to develop new products or to compete as vigorously as new companies that are still struggling to grow are often referred to as doing *tonosama shobai*. Large foreign companies that enter Japan and expect their size and the reputation they have in their own country to sustain them may also be accused of acting like *tonosama*. The accepted "Japanese way" is for all companies to don the apron of the traditional apprentice (*maedare*); assume a low, humble profile; and work diligently with a true, honest heart.

Tsugo ga warui-no de   (t'sue-go gah wah-rue-e-no day)—"Because of an inconvenience"—this is the most common excuse given for breaking an appointment or declining to go somewhere or do something when the individual can't or doesn't want to for whatever reason. No other explanation is given or expected.

Tsuketodoke   (t'sue-kay-toe-doe-kay)—The mid-year and year-end gifts that people give to their superiors and benefactors are known as *tsuketodoke*, which literally means "to deliver a bill," but in this case refers rather subtly to "paying off an obligation." *Tsuketodoke* play a significant role in maintaining business as well as personal relationships in Japan.

Tsumiawase   (t'sue-me-ah-wah-say)—This is translated as "company gifts" and refers to the gifts (liquor, fruit, etc.) that companies give to customers and connections in midsummer and at the end of the year to help maintain good working relations. The gifts are designed to smooth over any friction that might have developed during the preceding months and to express goodwill and appreciation. *Awase* by itself means "to adjust" or "to bring together" and in this context means to keep good relations on an even keel.

Tsuru no hitokoe (tsu-rue no ssh-toe-koe-eh) — When a group of Japanese in a company or organization is unable to reach a consensus on a topic or problem, the impasse is often broken by *tsuru no hitokoe* or "one word from a crane" — i.e., the president of the company or some other highly placed individual with authority that is unquestioned. The use of the phrase *tsuru no hitokoe* refers to the fact that when a flock of cranes lands to eat, one always stands guard and lets out a loud squawk if any danger approaches.

Uchi (uu-chee) — The word *uchi* literally means "inside" and is commonly used to mean house or home, but it is also synonymous with "our," "my," and "mine" and is used to draw very sharp distinctions between groups. *Uchi no kaisha*, for example, means "our company" or "my company." *Uchi no* by itself means it (or they) belongs to, is part of, my family or company or school or whatever group. Understanding the connotations and importance of *uchi* is essential to understanding the group orientation and behavior of the Japanese.

Uchi-age (uu-chee-ah-gay) — When the Japanese conclude an agreement following a period of negotiations or complete any project, they hold an *uchi-age* drinking party to celebrate the achievement and to reinforce feelings of camaraderie and cooperativeness. The term *uchi-age* actually means to "shoot off" (fireworks) or launch something such as a rocket, so the connotation is that the parties should be loud and lively.

Uchi-awase (uu-chee-ah-wah-say) — *Uchi-awase* literally means something like "to beat out an agreement" and by extension "to achieve harmony." The term, indispensable in Japan, is used to mean a planning session, and it applies to both business and recreation. Virtually all events, including meetings with foreign businessmen, are preceded by one or more *uchi-awase* during which the participants plan what they are going to do and how they are going to do it. *Uchi-awase* prior to negotiations with foreign companies may go on for days or even months and are very detailed.

Uka kosaku (uu-kah koe-sah-kuu) — To "fix something behind the scenes" is often applicable when one is petitioning the government for something or is negotiating a business deal — a common practice in Japan.

Undo-kai (uun-doe-kie) — Company *undo-kai* (athletic meets) are common in Japan and are part of the process of building fellowship and solidarity among employees and their families. Managers participate in the meets along with workers.

Wakarimashita (wah-kah-ree-mah-ssh-tah) — "I understand" or "understood." When the Japanese say *wakarimashita*, there is often an unstated "but" implied meaning that, while they understood what you said, they are not agreeing to anything.

Wah-puro (wah-puu-roe) — This is the Japanization of "word processor" and is "Japanese" as far as the Japanese are concerned. By the same process, a personal computer is a *paso kon* (pah-so kone) and a microcomputer is a *mai-kon* (my-kone).

Wa-kon! Yo-sai! (Wah-kone! Yoe-sie!) — This is a slogan that became popular in Japan during the Meiji period (1868-1912) when the Japanese first began their efforts to catch up with the West in technology and industry. It means "Japanese spirit! Western learning!"

Yakutoku (yah-kuu-toe-kuu) — These are gifts or other benefits that company employees receive because of their positions in their firms. The *yakutoku* are often from suppliers or others doing business with or wanting to do business with the recipient's company. *Yakutoku* may be in the form of gifts, travel, or entertainment. Such fringe benefits are traditional and are regarded as essential to maintaining good human relations, but if they are overdone, if their value is such that there is obviously an ulterior motive on the part of the giver, they may be regarded as an attempt to unduly influence the individual and be rejected. Knowing what constitutes an acceptable gift or benefit in kind is important. If the foreign businessman is in doubt, he should seek the advice of an experienced friend or advisor.

Yaku tsuki (yah-kuu t'sue-kee) — Literally "with title," this word refers to a person who has a title and is therefore a manager or executive. It can be used to mean anyone above the *sha-in* (company employee) level.

Yoroshiku (yoe-roe-she-kuu)—One of the most frequently used words in the Japanese language, this means "Please do whatever you can for me/us!" in any situation where you want someone else's cooperation, help, or goodwill. It is used in a multitude of situations, with the meaning varying to fit the circumstance, and is a strong, personal appeal. The full, polite phrase is *Yoroshiku onegaishimasu* (Yoe-roe-she-kuu oh-nay-guy-she-mahss).

Yukitsuke no ba (yuu-kee-skay no bah)—This is "favorite bar," and virtually all Japanese businessmen have one (or two or more). Establishing a relationship with bar managers, bartenders, and bar or club hostesses is one of the requirements of doing business in Japan, not only to avoid being taken by underworld-connected bars but also to assure good service when one entertains clients or subordinates, to demonstrate "face," and to be able to presume upon the goodwill and interest of the bar. Favorite bars are part of the individual businessman's network.

Yuryokusha (yuu-ree-yoe-kuu-shah)—"A person with influence," or someone who has enough clout or pull to get the son or daughter of a friend or relative a job in a desirable company, or to achieve some other goal or action.

Zaibatsu (zie-baht-sue)—"Financial clique," or a large industrial combine, often monopolistic in practice if not in principle. Ten or so of Japan's largest *zaibatsu* (Mitsui, Mitsubishi, C. Itoh, etc.) control over fifty percent of the country's import and export business.

Zaikai jin (zie-kie jeen)—*Zaikai* means something like "high finance" or "financial circles," and *jin* means "person." Combined, the word refers to a distinguished, generally wealthy, senior man, often retired from the highest levels of business or finance, who acts as a neutral counselor for major firms or groups involved in important deals. A variation of this term also used in reference to these high-level go-betweens is *zaikai shidosha* (she-doe-shah); *shidosha* means "leader" or "expert."

Zensho shimasu (zen-show she-mahss)—This is a term that frequently misleads and frustrates Western diplomats and politicians, as well as businessmen. It means "I will do my best," but sometimes it is translated as "I will take care of it," which is something altogether different. A Japanese prime minister once used the phrase to an American president, who was pressing him about something, and the U.S. president went back to Washington, D.C., believing he had a firm commitment. When the prime minister failed to deliver, the American president was very upset. Businessmen should keep in mind that the down side of "I will do my best" is "even though what you ask is impossible, I will do my best."